MS-DOS
Tips&Tricks

M. Tornsdorf
H. Tornsdorf

A Data Becker Book

First Printing, March 1990
Printed in U.S.A.

Copyright © 1990   Abacus
                      5370 52nd Street, S.E.
                      Grand Rapids, MI 49512

Copyright © 1989,1990 DATA BECKER GmbH
                       Merowingerstrasse 30
                       4000 Duesseldorf, West Germany

This book is copyrighted. No part of this book may be reproduced, stored in a retrieval system, or transmitted in any form or by any means, electronic, mechanical, photocopying, recording or otherwise, without the prior written permission of Abacus or Data Becker GmbH.

IBM, PC-AT, PC-XT, PC-BASIC and PC-DOS are trademarks or registered trademarks of International Business Machines Corporation. Microsoft Word, Multiplan, MS Windows, Excel, MS-DOS and GW-BASIC are trademarks or registered trademarks of Microsoft Corporation. Macintosh is a trademark or registered trademark of Apple Computer.

ISBN   1-55755-078-6

Foreword

If you ever wished you knew how to do any of the following:

- Alphabetically sort all the files on your hard disk, irrespective of the directories they are contained in?

- Find any file or key word on your hard disk or floppy diskette?

- Remove all files ending in BAK or TMP from every subdirectory of the hard disk?

- Save your eyes and the screen by shutting off the screen display without turning off the computer?

- Protect your files and directories or prevent strangers from having access to your computer?

- Back up your important data files and recover them in emergencies?

Then this is the book for you! Of course there is a lot more in this book than the examples we just listed. We just wanted to illustrate what we mean by "Tips and tricks" - practical solutions for routine MS-DOS problems.

What sort of MS-DOS background should you have

Don't worry about having an extensive computer background in MS-DOS to understand this book. This book isn't only for people that already know MS-DOS, but also for beginners. That's why we wrote this book for readers who had just finished our book "**MS-DOS For Beginners**". This book gives you more information to really start using your computer: an introduction to working with batch-files and tips you need to use GWBASIC and the DEBUG program to solve problems.

The tips and tricks can make your daily work a lot easier, even if you don't care about all the details of how they operate. If you can surprise your friends and relatives with what you learn from this book, so much the better. We had that in mind too.

The best way to use this book

Read the first chapter all the way through. You will find the necessary information for understanding the tips and tricks as well as advice on MS-DOS fundamentals. Then you can search through the remaining chapters and try out whatever you feel is most important or interesting to you. All of the tips and tricks are independent of one another so that you don't have to know one to use the other. You can also use the index or the special tip summary to find whatever you are looking for.

What we, as authors, would like from you, the reader

When you are working with this book you will soon notice that it really is about tips and tricks used to make daily work with the computer easier. We were able to achieve many of the things we first thought were impossible. There are probably a lot of other ideas waiting to be put into practice. Since we can't read your mind(s) it would be best if you simply wrote us a letter.

If you have ideas, suggestions or just want to give your opinion you can reach us at the following address: M. Tornsdorf, care of Abacus, 5370 52nd Street SE, Grand Rapids, MI 49512. Please include information about what you use your computer for as well as what kind it is. We hope you understand that we cannot answer every letter. However, we do take all of the suggestions into consideration. We wish you success with this book and working with MS-DOS.

May 1989
H. Tornsdorf
M. Tornsdorf
and all those who helped them in word and deed

Contents

Introduction 1
    Introduction to working with batch files..1
    If you have never worked with batch files..2
    Batch file programming 6
    Using path specifications 17
    Entering and using GWBASIC programs..18
    Machine language using debug..23

Batch file tips 25
    How to recognize batch file parameters 25
    Using system variables in batch files...26
    Using your own variables in batch files 28
    Temporary storage of multiple filenames..30
    Batch file warning messages 31
    Accessing your batch files..32
    Asking questions in a batch file...33

MS-DOS - Help messages..37
    MS-DOS commands with syntax and explanations.......................37
    Forbidding certain parameters in commands 40
    Creating your own help screens...42
    The ASCII chart at the press of a key 44

Displaying files and directories..47
    Optimum use of the DIR command...47
    Sorted directories 49
    Displaying directories that are correctly sorted 50
    How many bytes are in the directory?...54
    Displaying directory structure..56
    Searching for subdirectories 57
    All file names in alphabetical order 58

Contents

- Searching files 61
  - Searching for files in all of the directories.......................... 61
  - Searching files for specific text.. 62

- Working with multiple files 65
  - Using commands on all of the files of a disk drive 65
  - Selecting files with multiple criteria................................... 70
  - Searching the entire hard disk... 72
  - The easy way to search for text 73
  - Testing all of the files on the hard disk 74
  - Erasing files from the entire hard disk.................................. 75
  - Processing a directory with all of its subdirectories........... 76
  - Sorting all of the files in the correct path 76

- User and data protection 79
  - Has someone been using my computer?............................... 79
  - Who was the last person to use my computer? 81
  - How long did someone work on my computer? 84
  - How do you protect your computer while it's in use?.......... 85
  - How do you protect your computer from unwanted use?..... 87
  - How do you protect data and directories?............................ 87
  - How do you protect special files and directory names?..... 92
  - A completely hidden directory 93

- Printer Tips and Tricks 95
  - Print 132 or 80 characters per line.. 95
  - Adjusting various line spacings.. 97
  - Using a second printer port.. 97
  - Easy printer programming... 98
  - Does your printer print all the IBM characters?................. 101

- Screen Modes.. 103
  - Using character attributes to emphasize text..................... 103
  - Inverse Video.. 108
  - Setting character colors.. 109
  - Text or Graphic mode 111

- Keyboard Tips and Tricks... 113
  - Using a program to switch off Num Lock 113
  - Backslash assigned to the <F2> key..................................... 115
  - Escape sequences using COPY 117
  - Commands on the <Alt> key.. 119

Contents

Updating DOS 123
    Installation without a hard drive.. 123
    Installing DOS as a secondary version 124
    Installing a new version of DOS on the hard drive...................... 126
    Problem solving after installing a new DOS version 127

MS-DOS 4.0 Tips And Tricks 131
    Increasing keyboard speed... 131
    The mouse doesn't work in the DOS Shell 132
    Designing a new DOS Shell... 134
    Using functions from the original Shell in your Shell 136
    Linking any group to another Shell.. 137
    Adding as many groups as you want... 138
    Defining commands of any length in the DOS Shell 140
    User protection in MS-DOS 4.0... 141

Backing up data... 147
    Backing up data quickly and easily 149
    Using BACKUP properly.. 150
    The correct way to RESTORE 151
    Checking backup data with a control file..................................... 153
    Recovering data.. 155
    Analysis of a backup - What is on a backup diskette? 157
    Restoring files without using RESTORE...................................... 163

Quick Tips... 173
    Always available - COMMAND.COM 173
    Concealing executable programs.. 174
    Automatically saving data on a RAM disk.................................... 175
    Recovering the hard disk during FORMAT C:............................. 175
    Decreasing the number of files in the main directory................. 176
    Automatically avoiding error messages 177
    Expanding the PATH 178
    Prohibiting FORMAT C: - Protection by LABEL.......................... 179
    Protecting data from deletion... 180
    "Abort, Retry, Fail?"... 181
    "." and ".."... 182
    Tips on BUFFERS 183
    Longer names for directories 184
    Simple screen output... 184
    GWBASIC programs in the AUTOEXEC.BAT............................. 185
    Rapid disk copying using the hard disk 187
    Intercepting errors with ERRORLEVEL 188

Tips on DEL *.*	189
Protecting AUTOEXEC and CONFIG	190
Differences between COM, EXE and BAT files	192
Counting lines in files	193
Using commands on all the files in the directory	194
All files on the screen or printer	197
Skipping Prompts	197
Cold Boot from a batch file	198
Calling batch files from batch files (without CALL)	199
Invalid COMMAND.COM	201
Increasing environment memory (PATH, PROMPT, etc.)	202
Optimum use of the current directory	203
BACKUP and XCOPY tips	204
A DOS Prompt with Time, Date and Path	205
Exchanging data with an AT and an XT	208
Finding traces of old MS-DOS versions	209
40Mb hard disks - Saving data easily	210
Securing AT system data	211
Accessing the main directory with one key press	211
Protecting the screen with SCREEN.BAS	212
Aborting after incorrectly changing drives	212
Quickly deleting a command line	213
About the authors	215
Index	217

Introduction

We would like to keep this chapter as short as possible, since we are writing a book with many interesting tips and tricks and not a beginner's manual. Nevertheless, we can't exclude this chapter because we want to keep the individual subject areas separate from each other. You should be able to begin with whatever chapter you like. Since we don't want to repeat the basic information you will need in every chapter, we decided to cover the most important information in this chapter.

The only requirement for this book is the kind of know-how or knowledge you would have after reading **MS-DOS For Beginners**.

Introduction to working with batch files

Batch files are a vital tool that we use in many of our tips and tricks. They are easy to create. Because they are so helpful and important we would like to give you the following short summary.

We must distinguish between users that have never used batch files and users that have at least a fundamental knowledge of batch files. The first section is a simple, comprehensive introduction for users who have never worked with batch files. It introduces the fundamentals and functions of batch files. It also contains the most important rules for working with them.

The next part of the chapter summarizes the complicated rules for optimum operation of batch files. After reading it, beginners will be able to use the many example programs in this book without difficulty. Those who already know their way around batch files may wish to simply review these sections.

Introduction

If you have never worked with batch files

If you have never used batch files you should pay careful attention to this short introduction. This introduction briefly explains what a batch file is and what it can be used for. Simply read this introductory section.

Fundamentals and the significance of batch files

While the MS-DOS operating system is not always easy to use, it does provide you with many options which will always be available. However, you will come to the point where you are no longer satisfied with just entering a command from the keyboard and waiting for its execution. You will seem to be entering the same commands over and over again. Why not combine the MS-DOS commands in a list and then have them processed in one bundle? You call such a bundle of MS-DOS commands a batch file. Batch files have the extension BAT and you can call them like a program with the extension COM or EXE.

The AUTOEXEC.BAT file is a batch file

Even if you have never used a batch file before, there is one that you use without knowing it. The AUTOEXEC.BAT file has the commands that your computer executes when it's turned on (e.g. DATE or TIME on a computer without a built-in clock or it can set the system prompt). This is a group of MS-DOS commands that are AUTOmatically EXECuted when you turn your computer on. To check this, call the file with:

    AUTOEXEC

You may get an error message, depending on what your file looks like, because the AUTOEXEC program has already done what it is supposed to (when you turned on the computer). All the same, the principle of batch files should be clear. They can save us a lot of work by combining repeated commands into a single group.

Example: Batch files make it easy to enter commands

Let's start with a simple example. Certain MS-DOS commands require a lot of keyboard entry to achieve the desired results. You can write the same command in a batch file. Give it a name that is easy to call and you can save yourself a great deal of typing.

Let's assume you like to use the command DIR | SORT for sorting the directory, but hate typing in all those characters. You can use COPY CON to create the following batch file:

```
COPY CON DS.BAT
```

DS is a randomly selected abbreviation for "Directory, sorted". After entering this DOS command and pressing <Return>, write the DOS command on the screen the way you usually do. If your keyboard does not contain the pipe character, "|", (many international keyboards don't) you can use an <Alt> key combination (i.e. press down the <Alt> key and then <1>, <2> and <4> on the numeric keypad).

```
DIR A: | SORT
```

End the line by pressing the <Enter> key and store the new file by pressing the <F6> key. If you copy this file to a RAM DISK or the hard disk and set up the appropriate path (more about paths will be presented soon), the DS, directory sorted command will always be available.

As soon as you enter DS (plus the <Enter> key), the directory of the disk in drive A will be sorted and displayed. Make sure a diskette is in drive A.

Example: Using a batch file to go directly to a subdirectory

In our second example we assume that you have divided up your hard disk and have already created the fourth directory-level:

```
c:\texts\private\sport\handball
```

It can be very annoying if you have to spend a lot of time "moving through" to this subdirectory. It's a lot easier if you use the following batch called HANDBALL.BAT (or HB.BAT) to "jump right into the directory":

```
cd c:\texts\private\sport\handball
```

If you would like to view all of the files at the same time with the ending TXT, simply add the appropriate command:

```
DIR *.TXT
```

as the next line of your batch file. Now you have "batched" several command lines for the first time.

Introduction

Example: Calling programs with batch files

Another application of a one line batch file is calling a program from a subdirectory. For example, a batch file with the title WORD.BAT or W.BAT could read like this:

```
c:\prog\word4\word
```

You can also use alternatives with parameters. A batch file that loads the WORD word processor and the last text file processed by WORD with the name of WL.BAT (for WORD, last text) could contain the following line:

```
c:\prog\word4\word /l
```

Example: Calling two programs in the batch file

If you want you can load the mouse driver before calling the word processor. The appropriate batch file, that we named WM.BAT to distinguish it from other batch files, contains the following two lines. We are assuming that the driver is in the subdirectory mouse:

```
c:\mouse\mouse
c:\prog\word4\word
```

You can choose one of the two batch files depending on the situation.

Example: A BACKUP sequence using a batch file

Next, we are going to create a batch file that can process even more commands. This is a sequence of commands that can be useful in backing up a hard drive subdirectory that is directly below the main directory:

Use the following steps:

1. Backup a subdirectory with the BACKUP command using the /s option so that all the subdirectories contained in that subdirectory are copied. Be sure to create a LOG file by using the /l parameter. This /l parameter is only available in DOS 3.2 and above. This log file will contain a list of the files that were copied during the backup.

2. Copy and rename the LOG file onto one of the backup diskettes.

3. Copy it into a subdirectory of the hard disk (again with a new name that specifies the directory that the backup was performed on).

If you have never worked with batch files

4. You can erase the LOG file in the main directory.

As far as the name of the new log and batch file goes, "b33" indicates that you used the MS-DOS 3.3 BACKUP program to copy the files. "SD" stands for the subdirectory and must be changed in accordance with the directory you are backing up. "DISKLOG" refers to a subdirectory where the backup log files for various directories are stored.

If you want to try out this batch, please make sure that the directories SD and DISKLOG are present. A batch file with the name B33SD.BAT could contain the following lines. If you are using a version of DOS below 3.3, this procedure won't work since the /l option does not create the backup.log used in this batch file.

```
backup c:\sd\*.* a: /s/l
copy c:\backup.log a:b33sd.txt
copy c:\backup.log c:\disklog\b33sd.txt
del c:\backup.log
```

This is a very practical example of a batch file that you can design and modify to your own needs to make backing up selected files easy. The only problem is that we have to set up a special batch file for every subdirectory. You could use a word processor such as WORD to simplify things by exchanging SD for the name of the desired subdirectory and storing the new file under an appropriate name.

You can also write a batch file in such a way that the name of the object can be passed to the batch file.

Example: General batch file for erasing subdirectories

Suppose you wanted to erase an entire directory including all of its files after you have copied it. This is a lengthy, tiresome process. Why not use a batch file that first erases all the files in a subdirectory, then switches to the upper directory level and removes the subdirectory. After that, it displays the directory so you can check and select further subdirectories. Practice using this batch file only on floppy disks. DO NOT use it on a hard disk until you are familiar with its operation.

```
cd %1
del *.*
cd ..
rd %1
dir
```

If you store this batch file under the name DS.BAT (for delete subdirectory) and want to erase a subdirectory with the name of TEST, you can call the program from the corresponding upper directory with:

5

Introduction

        DS TEST

MS-DOS replaces %1 in the batch file with the parameter TEST. You must answer the delete prompt (which is sensible when you are deleting text). However, this is less work than entering all of the partial operations by hand.

Example: A backup batch file for passing names

Now we can redesign our backup batch file in such a way that we don't have to rewrite it for each subdirectory:

```
backup c:\%1\*.* a: /s/l
copy c:\backup.log a:b33%1.txt
copy c:\backup.log c:\disklog\b33%1.txt
del c:\backup.log
```

We store it under B33.BAT and can call it from the main directory with:

        B33 PROG

In this case, the subdirectory C:\PROG would be backed up with all of its subdirectories. In addition, you would save the corresponding LOG files.

Batch file programming

The following is a short review of batch file programming. All readers should review this information, you can skip over any information you are familiar with.

What are batch files

Batch files are special files (extension: BAT) that contain a series of DOS commands that are processed sequentially after you call the batch file. The most frequently used batch file is the AUTOEXEC.BAT. It automatically executes when you start the computer (cold or warm boot).

How do you create batch files

You can create batch files in many different ways because they are simple text files. It is important that they are stored in ASCII format, sometimes called text-only format. Remember to press the <Enter> key at the end of a command. The easiest method of creating a batch file is to copy it from the console (CON) with the MS-DOS command:

```
COPY CON NAME.BAT
```

This command enables you to write any number of MS-DOS commands into a batch file named NAME.BAT. Pressing the <F6> key will send DOS a control-Z character, which signifies the end of the file. The problem is that when you are using COPY CON you can only make corrections within one line. If you discover errors afterwards all you can do is retype the whole thing. That is why COPY CON is only suited for short batch files, although it is always available as a resident command.

The line editor, EDLIN, constitutes your second way of creating batch files. This is a transient DOS program that you have to read from a disk or the corresponding hard disk subdirectory.

EDLIN NAME.BAT starts the editor and opens or creates a file named NAME.BAT. Once the line editor is started a command prompt will be displayed on the left. The cursor will appear under the message "New File" next to an asterisk. You cannot enter any text in this command mode because the line editor is waiting for commands. Use <I> + the <Enter> key to insert new lines. Once in insert mode you enter the first line after the first line number. To get to the next line press the <Enter> key. Press <Ctrl> + <Z> or <F6> to exit the edit mode and the press <Enter> key to return to the command mode.

By entering a line number at the command mode (asterisk) you can display and re-enter it. Enter <E> to end the line editor and save the batch file.

The easiest way to enter your batch file is with a word processor that can save texts as an ASCII file (without any formatting or control commands). However, loading the word processor can be time consuming, especially if you don't have a hard disk.

Execute Sequence: COM/EXE/BAT

Files with the ending COM (command files) and EXE (executable program files) can be called and executed directly. Batch files with a BAT extension can call COM and EXE files. Remember that there is a set order of execution. Let's say you have a program called TEST.COM and a program called TEST.EXE in the same

Introduction

directory. If you write a batch file by the name of TEST.BAT in this directory and try to call it with:

    TEST

only TEST.COM will be executed. If this file has been erased, the program file TEXT.EXE will then execute. Only when this file disappears from the directory will you be able to call your TEST.BAT batch file. The easiest way to get around this problem is to give your batch files names that aren't being used for command and program files.

Batch File Commands: ECHO/At sign (@)

The command ECHO has two different tasks. If you enter a text after ECHO it will display the text to the current output device (usually the screen). You can use ECHO with the parameters ON and OFF to select whether or not the following command lines of the batch file should be displayed on the screen. Using ECHO without a parameter displays the immediate status (turned on or turned off).

To prevent the display of a batch file command on the screen you can (only with DOS 3.3 and above) place the @ character directly before the command. If you are using a version of DOS below 3.3, don't use the @ sign in your batch files, use the ECHO OFF command as the first line in the batch file. International keyboard users can produce the @ character by holding down the <Alt> key and pressing <6> and <4> on the numeric keypad. Release the <Alt> key and you will have the character @.

For example, this option is used if you want to have a batch file start with the command ECHO OFF. Although the following command lines will not display, the first command line will. You can prevent this by entering the following as your first line:

    @ECHO OFF

You can close the batch file at the end with:

    @ECHO ON

This only works on DOS 3.3 and above. If the @ECHO command is run on a version of DOS below 3.3, error messages will be displayed on the screen. Use this with caution if you wish to share your batch file with others.

REM

The REM command is another option used in batch files, you can add comments after REM. These comments won't be carried out, instead MS-DOS will skip over them or print them if ECHO is ON. This command will help you make your batch files more readable and understandable. The following programs give you examples.

Abort option

You can use <Ctrl> + <C> to abort a running batch file. MS-DOS will then ask:

```
End batch file (Y/N):
```

Depending on your answer the batch file will either abort or continue.

PAUSE

There is another method for interrupting a batch file that you can build into your own batch file.

What if you had a batch file that could help you erase all of the BAK files (BAcKup files) in your current directory? You may change your mind before finally erasing. The following program called DELB.BAT (for DEL BAK files) makes it possible for you to reconsider deleting the files. If you are using a version of DOS below 3.3, don't use the @ sign in your batch files, use the ECHO OFF command.

```
@ECHO Erase all files with the extension BAK.
@ECHO If this should not occur:
@ECHO Please abort with CTRL + C!
PAUSE
DEL *.BAK
```

The command PAUSE makes sure that MS-DOS waits at a given place for the press of a key before it continues processing the batch file.

Passing parameters

One special advantage of batch files is that you can construct them in a relatively general fashion and add special information as parameters when calling them. Such variable information is signified with a % sign and a number between 1 and 9 in a batch file. This makes 9 different parameters available for your use.

Introduction

To pass parameters to a batch file when calling it, write it like an MS-DOS command (i.e. after the name of the batch file separated by a space).

Here is an example: The following batch file REROUTE.BAT redirects the output of a command to a file. If you are using a version of DOS below 3.3, don't use the @ sign in your batch files.

```
@REM
@REM  | Batch for rerouting output to a file |
@REM
@ECHO off
%1 >\Output.dat %2 %3 %4 %5
@ECHO on
```

The parameters %2 to %5 can directly follow the %1. To draw a border around the comments of a batch file use the following characters. The numeric keypad and the <Alt> key are used to enter the character codes.

```
┌    <Alt> + <2> + <0> + <1>
═    <Alt> + <2> + <0> + <5>
┐    <Alt> + <1> + <8> + <7>
│    <Alt> + <1> + <8> + <6>
└    <Alt> + <2> + <0> + <0>
┘    <Alt> + <1> + <8> + <8>
```

First, create the REM lines with the border, then add the title and the actual command lines. Call the REROUTE.BAT file with a MS-DOS command that usually displays information to the screen. If there is no screen display, you will find a file named OUTPUT.DAT in the main directory. For example, if you call the REROUTE batch file with the DIR command as a parameter:

REROUTE DIR

you will then be able to look at the current directory with the command:

TYPE \Output.dat

When you write %1 in the batch as your first parameter, %1 will be replaced by the first given parameter when you start the batch file. You can check it on the screen by leaving the screen display on (No @ or ECHO OFF). You will then see the first parameter in every output command line containing %1.

After rerouting the output with ">\Output.dat", there are other parameters that can be passed on to the called command. You can transmit parameters such as /W (wide display in columns). Such a command line reads as follows:

    REROUTE DIR /W

FOR ... DO

You can use the command FOR ... DO to make loops so that portions of a batch file can be processed several times. The notation for this command is complex and will require a more detailed explanation.

We will start with two examples. First we will confine ourselves to a single direct entry, instead of using a batch file right away. A characteristic of the direct entry mode is the percentage sign.

    FOR %F IN (AUTOEXEC.BAT CONFIG.SYS) DO TYPE %F

F stands for file and represents a variable. After entering this line and pressing the <Enter> key the contents of the two files AUTOEXEC.BAT and CONFIG.SYS will be displayed on the screen, if they are available in the current directory. For the first time you can use the TYPE command on more than one file at the same time. With the line:

    FOR %F IN (*.BAT) DO TYPE %F

all the batch files in the current directory will be displayed on the screen. Here is the general form of an appropriate batch file line (notice the double percentage sign!):

    FOR %%V in (List) DO Command %%V

- %%V   This variable V (place holder) assumes all of the variables in the list, one after the other. You use only one percentage sign to enter this line directly into the command interpreter; you have to use two percentage signs for batch files. Always enclose the list in parentheses.

- *List*   Here you indicate which elements the command should be applied to. You can specify them (file1, file2, file3) or use a wild card (*.txt). In the first case the variable V contains file1, file2 and file3, one after the other, in the second case it contains all available files with the ending of .TXT.

Introduction

Command   After DO indicate the command that should be called each time for the new value.

GOTO

Using the command GOTO instructs MS-DOS to go to the label indicated after GOTO. The label has to be declared in the batch file with a colon and the label name.

While the following example is not very practical, it does show the principle:

```
@ECHO OFF
ECHO Now comes a jump
GOTO Mark
ECHO This place won't be reached
:Mark
ECHO MS-DOS branches here
@ECHO ON
```

The batch file skips over the line "ECHO This place won't be reached" and continues after the label ":Mark".

IF

You can use IF to check certain conditions. If the condition is fulfilled, the rest of the line after the condition will be processed. If the condition is not fulfilled it will go to the next line. Use a double equals sign "==" to check for equality. You can also use these key words with IF:

NOT condition   Reverses the condition.

EXIST file   Checks whether a file is available.

ERRORLEVEL   Contains the error message number of the last command processed. If there is no error, the ERRORLEVEL is 0.

The following example shows the application of the commands IF and GOTO. Our idea was: It would be nice if the parameters could be checked the same time a DOS command is entered. Then the user could be referred to the right syntax in cases where the wrong information has been entered. A batch file named TYPEM.BAT (for TYPE MORE) is ideal for this task. If you are using a version of DOS below 3.3, don't use the @ sign in your batch files, use the ECHO OFF command.

```
@REM
@REM   This batch outputs a text file a page at a time
@REM
@IF "%1" == "" GOTO Syntax
@IF NOT EXIST %1 GOTO Not_there
@TYPE %1 | MORE
@GOTO End
:Syntax
@ECHO This batch file outputs a text file page by page
@ECHO File name must be given
@GOTO End
:Not_there
@ECHO The file does not exist!!!
@GOTO End
:End
```

The example program checks for two possible errors in operation:

1. If no parameter is given when the program is called, the program branches to the label "Syntax". This section of the batch file displays the function of the batch file and the proper call. Then the batch file ends.

    Tip: If you have questions concerning the line:

    `@IF "%1" == "" GOTO Syntax`

    refer to the chapter "How to recognize batch file parameters".

2. If a parameter has been given, but no file of the same name is found, the batch file informs you of this and then ends.

Here is another example of the application of the commands IF and GOTO, that also takes us to another command (SHIFT).

Sometimes it is important to be able to determine the quantity of given parameters and react accordingly. There is a little trick that makes this very easy.

If you want to process every given parameter in a batch file you could write all of the parameters with the appropriate commands. Let's assume you want to write a batch that will display all given files on the screen. Then the batch file could look like the following. If you are using a version of DOS below 3.3, don't use the @ sign in your batch files, use the ECHO OFF command:

Introduction

```
@REM TYPEDAT.BAT
@REM
@REM  | Batch for outputting given files |
@REM
@ECHO off
IF "%1" == "" GOTO End
TYPE %1
PAUSE
IF "%2" == "" GOTO End
TYPE %1
PAUSE
IF "%3" == "" GOTO End
TYPE %3
:End
@ECHO on
```

Not only is this batch long, it can only display the three given files. The following command will make your batch files a lot more flexible and user friendly.

SHIFT

You know that you can give parameters after the filename when calling a batch file, separated by a space, using %1 to %9. Shift allows you to use more than 10 parameters in the batch file. Using the command word SHIFT you can copy the contents of the variables %1 to %9 "a parameter deeper". This causes the contents of %9 to shift to %8, the contents of %8 to shift to %7, and so on while the contents of the variable %0 are lost. The 10th parameter is now available under %9.

Now we are going to take advantage of this shifting of parameters by modifying our last batch file example. We call it TYPEDAT.BAT.

```
@REM TYPEDAT.BAT
@REM
@REM  | Batch for outputting given files |
@REM
@ECHO off
:Continue
IF "%1" == "" GOTO End
TYPE %1
PAUSE
SHIFT
GOTO Continue
:End
@ECHO on
```

The trick in this batch file is the processing of only the parameter %1 in a loop. To process all existing parameters, you use the command SHIFT to move all of the parameters to the place holder %1. That is: %2 becomes %1. At the same time all available "higher" parameters are "shifted down" by one. The batch file checks each time whether the next parameter is given or empty. If the next parameter is empty it branches to the end of the batch file.

Calling a batch file from a batch file: Call

You can use CALL to call other batch files as subroutines. This works with MS DOS Version 3.3 and above. With the older versions of MS-DOS you have to call a new command interpreter with COMMAND /C instead of using CALL to execute other batch files.

To illustrate this we will change our last batch file TYPEDAT.BAT so that the individual files will no longer be output with TYPE. Instead, the batch file TYPEM.BAT will do it. You will find TYPEM.BAT after the explanation of the command IF.

```
@REM TYPEDAT.BAT
@REM
@REM   Batch for outputting given files
@REM
@ECHO off
:Continue
IF "%1" == "" GOTO End
REM Now comes the changed line, DOS 3.3 and above only!!!
CALL TYPEM %1
PAUSE
SHIFT
GOTO Continue
:End
@ECHO on
```

Prevent errors: illegal characters

Have you ever called a batch file that you wrote yourself, only to have strange things happen? You could have used special characters that are illegal in batch files.

There are some characters that you either can't use or that you can't use very easily in batch files. They are:

%   MS-DOS uses this character for designating the parameters %1 to %9. To use this character in the text (for example to output with ECHO), you have to print it twice (%%).

Introduction

<   The character "<" redirects the input from the normal keyboard to a new device or file. You cannot use this character in a batch file or display it on the screen.

\>   This character redirects the output to a different device than the screen and is illegal in batch files.

| This character transmits program output to another program (filter). This character is also illegal in batch files.

If you must display the characters "< >" or "|" in a batch file, then write the screen output in a separate file and use the command COPY to copy the file onto the screen. Suppose you wanted to display the line:

```
The characters "< > |" are illegal
```

on the screen. Write this line in the file ILLEGAL.DAT and use the following command in your batch file:

```
COPY ILLEGAL.DAT CON
```

The reason the characters "< > |" produce such strange effects is because MS-DOS always carries out the corresponding action for these characters, even if they are within a screen display or follow REM as comments. The following batch file, TEST.BAT, produces a particularly interesting effect:

```
REM This is a | test
```

If you call this batch file (it has to be named TEST.BAT) the REM line will appear over and over on the screen until you use <Ctrl> + <C> to abort. MS-DOS will then ask:

```
End batch file (Y/N):
```

Enter "Y" to end the batch file. MS-DOS uses the character "|" to call the program that follows (TEST - the same batch file) over and over again.

Using path specifications

The PATH command is important when working with MS-DOS and especially when working with the ideas of this book. PATH refers to the search path of the drives and possible directories that MS-DOS will search to find a certain command or file.

If you didn't give a PATH, MS-DOS will first check whether the command is resident, for example DIR or DATE. Then it will search the current drive and directory for an appropriate program or file.

If you want to have MS-DOS make use of all the capabilities in your batch file directory, you must give it the appropriate path reference. The best way to do this is to put it into the AUTOEXEC.BAT file.

Define a path as a direct command or within the AUTOEXEC.BAT file, by giving the appropriate drive and directory after the PATH command. For example, you could enter:

    PATH C:\BAT

Besides this you can enter several search paths, separated by a semicolon, that will be evaluated in the corresponding sequence. For example:

    PATH C:\DOS;C:\BAT;C:\WORD

In this case MS-DOS would first search in the current directory, then in the DOS directory (e.g. for FORMAT.COM), then in your batch file directory and finally in your word processing directory, if it was named WORD.

If the example batch files don't work, you could have specified the wrong search path. MS-DOS would then be unable to find what you're looking for. You can use the DOS command PATH, without any parameters to display the current path specifications.

To add a path you have to re-enter all partial paths or use the quick tip in this book that introduces the special batch file ADDPATH.

Introduction

Remember the sequence that MS-DOS follows when executable files have the same name and differ only in their extensions. First comes COM, next EXE and then the files with the extension BAT.

Entering and using GWBASIC programs

Batch files and MS-DOS commands can't do all the work necessary to get the most out of MS-DOS. Programming languages offer many enhanced solutions. Therefore, it would be a shame to do without the practical solutions these languages offer.

We decided to fall back on the programming language GWBASIC, which usually comes with MS-DOS. Since we can't assume that you have already programmed with GWBASIC, this is a list of the information necessary to run the programs mentioned in this book. You will find that it is easy to understand and that the programs, in view of their performance, are very short.

How do I load and start GWBASIC?

Check your DOS diskette(s) or look in your DOS directory to see whether you have GWBASIC and to find out where it is. We found it with:

    DIR C:\DOS\GW*.*

on the hard disk:

    GWBASIC EXE   80608 06.10.88   0.00

You may wish to write a batch file named GW.BAT or BAS.BAT to call GWBASIC to make things easier. After calling GWBASIC a screen similar to the following will appear, yours may differ slightly.

Entering and using GWBASIC programs

```
GW-BASIC 2.02
(C) Copyright Microsoft 1983,1984

AT&T Personal Computer  Release 2.1
Copyright (c) 1984 by AT&T, all rights reserved

Compatibility Software
Copyright (c) 1984 by Phoenix Software Associates Ltd.

61885 Bytes free
Ok█




                                                                            



 1LIST   2RUN   3LOAD"  4SAVE"  5CONT  6,"LPT"  7TRON  8TROFF 9KEY    0SCREEN
```

Fig. 1·   *GWBASIC*

How do I enter program lines in GWBASIC?

To use one of our GWBASIC programs in this book copy the lines from the book. Pay attention to detail; especially the blank spaces. You also have to confirm every line you enter by pressing the <Enter> key.

The numbers at the beginning of each line give the sequence in which the program lines should be processed. For practical reasons we chose intervals of ten. This allows you to add lines later without a lot of trouble.

If you make a mistake typing, you can correct it in the line. Use the <Insert> key to change between the insert and overtype modes. Remember that changes are "valid" only after you have pressed the <Enter> key.

How do I check program lines?

To check your program, use:

   LIST <Enter> key

to display the entire program. You can also enter specific program lines after LIST, for example:

19

Introduction

```
LIST 20 - 60
```

Don't be surprised that GWBASIC converts lowercase letters to uppercase. This only demonstrates that GWBASIC has recognized a command and indicates this by capitalizing the letters.

How do I save a GWBASIC program?

To save the program enter the following command (place the cursor on a free line!):

```
SAVE "name"
```

"name" represents the program name you selected. We recommend that you follow our suggestions.

Starting and interrupting programs

To start a program enter the command:

```
RUN
```

in a free line. To interrupt a program use either <Ctrl> + <C> or <Ctrl> + <Break>. You should save the program before starting it so that an error or unexpected reaction (crash) of the program won't destroy your work. For example, if you give the SYSTEM command to exit GWBASIC before saving your work, all of your work will be lost. If you didn't save the program beforehand it will be lost.

How do I end GWBASIC?

To end GWBASIC (after saving the program) enter the following command in a free line and press the <Enter> key.

```
SYSTEM
```

How do I load and change a program?

To load and change a program, load GWBASIC and type the following command into a free line:

```
LOAD "name"
```

Then you can use:

```
LIST
```

to display the program on the screen, move the cursor to the line and change it. Remember that changes are only accepted after you have pressed the <Enter> key while in the appropriate line.

How do I call a GWBASIC program?

To call and execute a GWBASIC program simply enter the name of the program (without the extension BAS) after GWBASIC, for example:

```
GWBASIC NAME
```

What do I do when there's an error message?

After starting a BASIC program you might get an error message. Most likely the error message will be:

```
Syntax error in xxx
```

For xxx, GWBASIC displays the line number where the error was discovered. At the same time the line is displayed and (depending on the version of BASIC you have) the cursor will flash at the place where GWBASIC thinks the error is located.

If this happens, compare the line with the line in the book. You will probably notice a slight difference. Correct the line and complete the change with the <Enter> key.

Other error messages, which do not provide a line number, may also appear. In these instances you must compare the entire program with the typed version.

If GWBASIC should report a syntax-error in a correct line that contains the BASIC command SHELL, this means that you have an older version of BASIC. Replace it with a new version as soon as possible.

Compiling GWBASIC programs

GWBASIC is an interpreter, which means that after you start a program with RUN, GWBASIC first interprets the program and then executes the program, line for line, command for command. The program isn't checked until you start it. Unlike GWBASIC, there are BASIC compilers that don't immediately start a program. Instead the compiler first checks and translates the program into machine language, usually storing it in the translated form, before the program can start.

Introduction

There are advantages and disadvantages to having interpreters and compilers. Interpreters are usually slow, although GWBASIC might seem fast to you. The reason they are so slow is that they check and translate while the program is running, which is time consuming. Also, certain parts of the program might be translated many times. For example, in the loop:

```
10 FOR i = 1 to 1000
20 PRINT I
30 NEXT I
```

line 20 is checked and translated 1000 times, that is, every time GWBASIC executes this line. An interpreter is helpful for beginning programmers because it is very easy to make changes and to test them.

A compiler would only translate these three program lines once. So the program can be executed much faster. However, translating into machine language often takes up a lot of time, and the compiler requires this amount of time every time you change the program.

Another advantage of compiled programs (programs translated by a compiler) is that they can be started without GWBASIC, like MS-DOS commands. Also, they can't be changed by users or viewed with LIST.

You might be wondering why we are telling you all this, since GWBASIC is an interpreter. However, GWBASIC also has a compiler, the QuickBASIC compiler, manufactured by Microsoft. So if GWBASIC is too slow for you or if you want to use the BASIC programs from this book without GWBASIC, consider this compiler. We compiled all of the programs in this book for our own purposes and we recommend that you do the same.

Machine language using debug

Don't worry. We are not going to introduce you to the mysteries of machine language. However, there are a few tricks and solutions that require some machine language (i.e. where batch files and BASIC programs can't help). You'll barely notice the difference between our solutions and tricks using machine language and the other solutions.

What is machine language

Machine language is your computer's "native tongue". Although your PC requires a "translator" to understand BASIC, it is able to understand and execute machine language. It's only people who have a hard time understanding and using machine language.

How do I create a machine language program

Just as you would use COPY CON, an editor is needed to enter batch files and the program GWBASIC is needed to work with BASIC. Help is also required to enter machine language programs.

The program DEBUG provides this help. The name means to remove bugs or errors. You can also use DEBUG to view and change memory contents in your PC as well as have DEBUG run your program; you can even create your own machine language programs with DEBUG. The MS-DOS system diskette that came with your computer contains the DEBUG program. If you have a hard disk the DEBUG program may be in the DOS directory.

If you start DEBUG as you would any other MS-DOS command, the screen will only show a small, horizontal line that, like EDLIN, asks you to enter commands.

For example, you could enter the command that enables you to create a machine language program. To leave DEBUG again, simply enter "Q" (for QUIT) after the horizontal line. This ends your work with DEBUG.

How to enter our machine language programs

The following solution should help you enter our small programs without encountering too much machine language.

We will enter all of the commands necessary for creating the machine language program in the same way we created our batch files (for example using COPY CON, EDLIN or your word processor). This will keep you on familiar ground so you will be able to make changes easily.

Store this command sequence for DEBUG like a batch file. In order for DEBUG to process this command sequence you have to redirect the input to this file with the "<" sign when you call DEBUG. The last character in the command file is the character "Q", which causes the computer to automatically leave DEBUG. As a result, DEBUG creates the executable program for you before leaving.

Don't worry if this sounds complicated, it isn't. The first machine language example program will show you how easy it is.

Errors when using DEBUG

In our procedure it is vital that you enter everything exactly the way it is typed in the book, including spaces. Otherwise DEBUG may give you an error message (although DEBUG gets its commands from the file, its messages still go to the screen) while waiting for further instructions from the previously created file. If this happens, abort DEBUG with <Ctrl> + <Break> and compare your DEBUG command file with the typed version in the book. The companion diskette for this book also contains all of the machine language source code and executable programs.

Batch file tips

How to recognize batch file parameters

The problem

It is often very important to find out whether the user gave all of the necessary parameters when a batch file was called. This makes it possible to react accordingly in the batch file.

The solution

To guarantee that the necessary parameters are given when the batch file is called, use the following line in your batch file:

```
IF "%1" == "" GOTO NoParam
```

You have to define a label for this in your batch file:

```
:NoParam
ECHO You have to give a parameter
GOTO END
```

If your batch file requires more than one parameter, use (IF "%1" == "" GOTO NoParam) for all of the necessary parameters (%2, %3 ...).

Explanation

It isn't necessary to use quotation marks for parameters such as %1. To determine whether or not a parameter has been given or if the accompanying variable doesn't have any contents use the following line:

```
IF %1 ==    GOTO Error
```

MS-DOS will then give the error message "Syntax Error!", because there wasn't anything to compare it with. You can get around this by putting quotation marks on both sides of the equals signs. For example, if the parameter had the contents Text.txt the comparison would be:

```
IF "Text.txt" == "" GOTO NoParam
```

The condition hasn't been fulfilled. Only if parameter 1 is "empty", will the line read:

```
IF "" == "" GOTO NoParam
```

Now the condition is fulfilled and MS-DOS will branch to the label NoParam.

Using system variables in batch files

The problem

Since MS-DOS is flexible, you can easily make it fit your own needs. The introduction of system variables has contributed to MS-DOS' flexibility. You can change these system variables from batch files.

The solution

Use the command SET to display all of the currently defined system variables. There are usually three defined variables:

PROMPT   Contains the system prompt.

Using system variables in batch files

COMSPEC   Contains the path and the name of the command interpreter; in certain cases you have to reload the command interpreter. MS-DOS requires these specifications to reload the command interpreter.

PATH   Contains the entire path specification. All of the individual directories listed here are searched for a given program.

These variables are also referred to as environmental variables because they define the environment in which MS-DOS operates. You can use these variables from batch files and change them at will. The following batch file checks whether a command interpreter has been set with COMSPEC and if not it will set it. If you are using a version of DOS below 3.3, don't use the @ sign in your batch files.

```
@REM
@REM  | Batch file for setting the command interpreter |
@REM
@ECHO off
IF NOT "%COMSPEC%" == "" GOTO CONTINUE
SET COMSPEC=C:\COMMAND.COM
ECHO Command-interpreter set to C:\COMMAND.COM
:CONTINUE
@ECHO on
```

Explanation

To use an environmental variable in a batch file, put the name between percentage signs. To determine whether COMSPEC is available, we will compare "%COMSPEC%" to "". If COMSPEC has been set as an environmental variable the batch will terminate by jumping to CONTINUE, otherwise it will use the MS-DOS command SET to set a standard value for COMSPEC.

Batch file tips

Using your own variables in batch files

The problem

Often the parameters and system variables given by the user are not enough for a batch file. For example, the batch file could require its own variables to put certain results in temporary storage for use at a later date.

The solution

You can use the MS-DOS command SET to define new variables as environmental variables and remove them later. The following example changes the prompt in such a way that time, date, path and MS-DOS version are displayed while keeping the original prompt available.

```
@REM SETPRMPT.BAT
@REM
@REM   Batch file for modification of the prompt
@REM
@SET OLDPROMPT=%PROMPT%
@PROMPT Date:$l$d$g Time:$l$t$g $_Path:$l$p$g $_Version:$l$v
@SET PROMPT=%OLDPROMPT%
@SET OLDPROMPT=
```

Tip: You may get the following error message when you enter and start the example:

```
Out of environment space
```

Simply add a line in your CONFIG.SYS file:

```
SHELL=C:\COMMAND.COM /P /E:990
```

For C:\COMMAND.COM enter the path and name of the command interpreter you are using. This will increase the storage capacity of the environmental memory from 127 to 990 bytes. You can use a greater value, for example 2000 bytes.

Caution: This modification does not go into effect until the next time you start your PC. You can also start the command interpreter with a new value

for the environmental memory by entering the following line after the prompt:
COMMAND /P /E:990

You can only do this if you haven't reloaded the current command interpreter from another program. In WORD this happens with "ESC <L>ibrary <R>un COMMAND" or in the MS-DOS 4.0 Shell with the first menu entry or <Shift> + <F9>. In both of these cases you can use EXIT to get back, unless you use the given line. If you haven't left a program to run the command interpreter you can use the command.

Explanation

Using SET OLDPROMPT=%PROMPT% you can define a new environmental variable with the name OLDPROMPT and can assign it to the current prompt. That way you save the current prompt and can recover it later.

The next line, @PROMPT Date:ld$g Time:$ltg $_Path:$lpg $_Version:$l$v, defines a new prompt. The data following the dollar sign is not displayed directly, but replaced by the following contents:

$l   Displays the sign "<".

$g   Displays the sign ">". $l and $g are used to make the desired data stand out.

$d   Displays the current date.

$t   Displays the time.

$_   Ends the line and begins a new line. This makes the display clearer.

$p   Displays the drive and path.

$v   Displays the version of MS-DOS.

The blank line ensures that the newly defined prompt will be displayed on the screen. We prevented all of the other command lines from being displayed on the screen with the character "@". So only the desired data is displayed on the screen.

We use the line SET PROMPT=%OLDPROMPT% to give the environmental variable PROMPT the old value previously stored in OLDPROMPT. This is enough to define a new (that is, the old prompt) prompt. You won't even need the MS-DOS command PROMPT.

The last line SET OLDPROMPT= removes the variable we set up from the environmental memory so that there is room again.

Temporary storage of multiple filenames

The problem

A single batch file can't always process all of the necessary information needed to perform certain tasks. Sometimes the information has to go into temporary storage. A batch file can set up files for this.

The solution

Simply use the redirection character ">" to redirect the desired data. Later on you can continue processing this data. The following batch file shows the technique, which leads to quicker results.

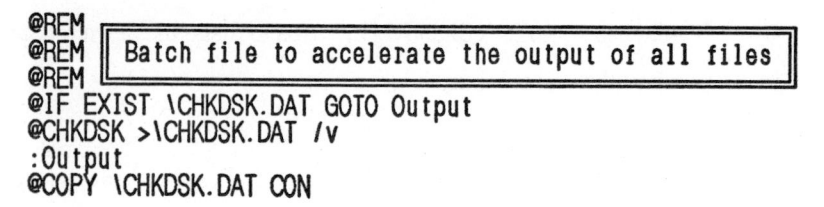

```
@REM
@REM   Batch file to accelerate the output of all files
@REM
@IF EXIST \CHKDSK.DAT GOTO Output
@CHKDSK >\CHKDSK.DAT /v
:Output
@COPY \CHKDSK.DAT CON
```

The first time you call this batch it will take a long time for the files to be displayed on the screen. If your computer seems to hang up, CHKDSK has found errors on the disk, press <Ctrl> + <C> to exit. Check your DOS manual for instructions on using CHKDSK. After the first time, the output will increase in speed because the information won't have to be recalculated, it will only have to be read out of a file.

Explanation

You can use the CHKDSK command to check the data diskette or hard disk. The "/v" parameter is used to display all of the checked files. This is a very simple way of looking at the entire contents of a disk or hard disk with all of the subdirectories. We will go into more detail in the chapter "Searching for files" (i.e. how to use CHKDSK to find a file). Since it takes a long time to check all of the files, the screen display of the CHKDSK command is redirected to the file CHKDSK.DAT the first time, and every call after that displays only this file.

Tip: Every time you create new files or erase old ones it means that the contents of the file CHKDSK.DAT are no longer identical to the contents of the drive. Erase this file so that a new one can be created.

Batch file warning messages

The problem

Some batch files do dangerous, but important work. For example, a batch file could easily erase all temporary files with the ending .TMP. For safety reasons you should be informed of this procedure before the batch file starts erasing them.

The solution

It is easy to inform the user about potentially dangerous operations: Use the ECHO command to inform you of what the batch file is doing and then use the PAUSE command. Press any key to continue the program or press <Ctrl> + <C> to abort it. The following example erases all files ending in TMP from the current directory at the press of a key:

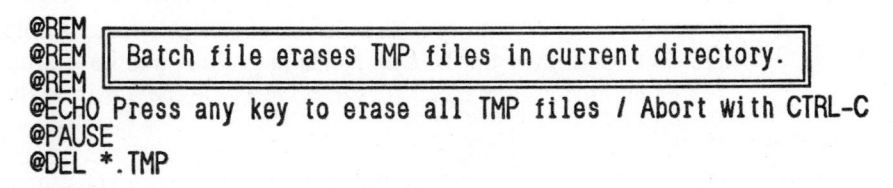

```
@REM
@REM   Batch file erases TMP files in current directory.
@REM
@ECHO Press any key to erase all TMP files / Abort with CTRL-C
@PAUSE
@DEL *.TMP
```

Explanation

The PAUSE command displays the message "Strike a key when ready" and waits for the press of a key. You can abort the batch with <Ctrl> +<C>. The message:

```
Terminate batch job (Y/N)?
```

will be displayed. Enter "Y" to end the batch file. Remember to press and hold down the <Ctrl> key and then press the <C> key to abort, otherwise the batch file will interpret the pressed <C> as "press any key" and continue processing.

Accessing your batch files

The problem

While reading this book you will probably discover interesting batch files that you will want to use regularly. You should make sure that you can always access these batch files, no matter what directory you are currently in.

The solution

The method for getting immediate access to batch files depends on your computer equipment:

1. If you have a PC with a floppy disk drive then you probably need most of the space on the MS-DOS diskette for MS-DOS commands. That doesn't leave much room for batch files. If your system has more than 512 Kilobytes of memory, you can set up a RAM disk and copy batch files to it. Define a path for the RAM disk so that you can directly access the batch files.

2. If you have a PC with two disk drives you could, for example, have the MS-DOS diskette with the commands in drive A and have a diskette with further commands and batch files in drive B. Define a path to the batch file for drive B.

3. The easiest, most convenient method is to use batch files with a hard disk. Create the directory C:\BAT, and copy all batch files to the new directory. Expand the path in the AUTOEXEC.BAT file to include this directory and you will be able to call batch files from any directory, just like MS-DOS commands.

Asking questions in a batch file

The problem

You can't always give a batch file all of the necessary information with parameters. Sometimes a batch file has to ask for additional information. Also, you may wish to confirm the operation before continuing with the batch file.

The solution

An easy way to solve this is if you have the commercial program *Norton Utilities* that contains a program called ASK.EXE that solves this problem. Copy this program into the BAT directory so that it can be used by all of the batch files. The following example shows how to use ASK.EXE:

```
@REM
@REM    Batch for asking questions with Nortons ASK.EXE
@REM
@ECHO "I will now ask something"
@ASK "Y/N",YN
@IF ERRORLEVEL 2 GOTO N
@IF ERRORLEVEL 1 GOTO Y
@GOTO end
:Y
@ECHO "Y"
@GOTO end
:N
@ECHO "N"
@GOTO end
:end
```

Even if you don't have *Norton Utilities* there is an easy solution. You need a small machine language program that has a comparable function. You don't need any special knowledge to create this program, it is really easy. Enter the following lines using COPY CON ASK.DEB or with an editor (for example EDLIN) under the filename ASK.DEB:

Batch file tips

```
A
MOV AX,0C07
INT 21
MOV AH,4C
INT 21

RCX
9
nASK.COM
W
Q
```

After saving the file, call the MS-DOS command DEBUG by entering the following line:

```
DEBUG <Ask.DEB
```

If everything was entered correctly, DEBUG will take its input from the ASK.DEB file and create a machine language program. You will then have a small executable program, ASK.COM, which can be used in the following way:

```
@REM ASKONE.BAT
@REM
@REM   Batch for asking questions with ASK.COM
@REM
ECHO OFF
:Input
ECHO (y)es or (n)o ?
ASK
IF ERRORLEVEL 121 GOTO Yes
IF ERRORLEVEL 110 GOTO No
GOTO Input
:Yes
IF ERRORLEVEL 122 GOTO Input
ECHO Yes
GOTO End
:No
IF ERRORLEVEL 111 GOTO Input
ECHO No
GOTO End
:End
@ECHO ON
```

You can use other characters instead of "y" and "n" to ask questions by using the appropriate ASCII code after ERRORLEVEL. However, you must ask the ERRORLEVELS in descending sequence.

Explanation

The machine language program that you created with the help of DEBUG waits for the input of a character and returns the ASCII value of the character as an error code. You can only ask for the value within the batch file using ERRORLEVEL. The condition is fulfilled if ERRORLEVEL is larger or equal to the value given after it. This is why the highest value is checked first. The batch file checks, in descending sequence, whether the return value is greater than or equal to the value of the character to be checked. Then it uses GOTO to branch to the proper place if necessary.

Then the batch checks whether the ERRORLEVEL is greater than the ASCII value of the character. If the batch didn't do this, you could enter "o" (ASCII 111) instead of "n" because the value would not be equal to but greater than 110 ("n").

MS-DOS - Help messages

MS-DOS contains many commands that require many different parameters. It is almost impossible to remember every command and all of their parameters. You'll probably have to look up many commands in the manual when first working with MS-DOS. In this section we will show you how to display help information on the screen any time you like.

We will give you some tips on how to install online help screens to the DOS commands. Every DOS command will show the exact syntax after you call it.

MS-DOS commands with syntax and explanations

The problem

There are times you forget how to call commands that you don't use very often. You might also want to use a certain option but can't remember the name for it. MS-DOS can help you a lot faster than it would take for you to find the answer in the manual.

The solution

You need three things to have MS-DOS help you:

1. A directory for batch files, in which you can put the auxiliary batch files.

MS-DOS - Help messages

2. A path for this directory, so that you can find these files among all the directories later. When using the PATH command remember to enter the directory with the batch files first, then enter the DOS directory. Here is an example of the correct path specification:

PATH C:\BAT;C:\DOS

3. A separate batch file is required for each command with which you need help.

We'll use the FORMAT command to illustrate what this type of batch help file (FORMAT.BAT) should look like. If you are using a version of DOS below 3.3, don't use the @ sign in your batch files. Use the ECHO OFF command instead.

```
@ECHO off
@REM FORMAT.BAT
@REM
@REM  | FORMAT-Help |
@REM
IF "%1" == "/?" GOTO Help
C:\DOS\FORMAT %1 %2 %3 %4 %5 %6 %7 %8 %9
GOTO End
:Help
ECHO
ECHO  | FORMAT {DD:} {/o}{/v}{/1}{/4}{/8}{/s}{/b}{/n:xx}{/t:yy}
ECHO  | DD Disk drive label
ECHO  | /o    : MS DOS 1.x Format
ECHO  | /v    : With name input (Disk label)
ECHO  | /1    : One side
ECHO  | /4    : 360 KB two sided
ECHO  | /8    : 8 Sectors
ECHO  | /s    : Copy system
ECHO  | /b    : Leave room for system
ECHO  | /n:xx : Number of sectors/track ——\ use together
ECHO  | /t:yy : Number of tracks/page   ——/ track and sector
ECHO
:End
@ECHO on
```

To use the FORMAT command, simply call it as you normally would. For example:

FORMAT A:

If you want any help from any help batch file simply use a question mark as your parameter. For example:

FORMAT /?

The result of the batch file will then look like this:

```
C:\BOOKS\DOS_PROD>format /?

C:\BOOKS\DOS_PROD>ECHO off

FORMAT {DD:} {/o}{/v}{/1}{/4}{/8}{/s}{/b}{/n:xx}{/t:yy}
DD Disk drive label
 /o    : MS DOS 1.x Format
 /v    : With name input (Disk label)
 /1    : One side
 /4    : 360 KB two sided
 /8    : 8 Sectors
 /s    : Copy system
 /b    : Leave room for system
 /n:xx : Number of sectors/track DDDDD\ use together
 /t:yy : Number of tracks/page   DDDDD/ track and sector

C:\BOOKS\DOS_PROD>
```

Fig. 2:   Help with the FORMAT command

Explanation

When you enter a command, MS-DOS will search for the desired command in all directories indicated by the PATH statement. The directories will be processed in the order which they appear in the path statement. If the C:\BAT directory is the first directory that is indicated, MS-DOS will find the desired FORMAT command, but as a batch file. So MS-DOS won't execute the proper command in the DOS directory.

The batch file, FORMAT.BAT, specifies the whole path to call the MS-DOS program FORMAT, otherwise MS-DOS will find the batch file first again. Which would lead to an infinite loop.

Note: Calling this batch file for help won't work if C:\DOS is the current directory because MS-DOS will search for the program in the current directory first and then it will consider path specifications.

To be able to call for help in the DOS directory you would have to rename all of the MS-DOS commands (for example by placing an underline "_" before the command) and then change the line in the batch file by calling the original program in the following way:

C:\DOS_FORMAT %1 %2 %3 %4 %5 %6 %7 %8 %9

39

Suggestion

The following are the DOS commands for which you should create batch help files.

    FORMAT
    BACKUP
    RESTORE
    PRINT
    MODE
    XCOPY
    EDLIN
    CHKDSK
    FIND

Forbidding certain parameters in commands

The problem

Certain MS-DOS commands can sometimes be very harmful. Two examples of this are the FORMAT command with the parameter "C:" or the command "DEL *.*". After long hours of work you could accidentally enter one of those commands, which could cause much damage. What if you could simply forbid certain parameters in commands?

The solution

Setting up auxiliary batch files for MS-DOS commands enables you to ask for certain parameters and if necessary, abort them. We will demonstrate this with the FORMAT command, but we will use "B:" instead of "C:" because it is not as dangerous. For that purpose we will expand our help batch file with the following lines:

    IF "%1" == "b:" GOTO Forbid
    IF "%1" == "B:" GOTO Forbid

The entire program would then look like this:

```
@ECHO OFF
@REM HFORMAT.BAT
@REM
@REM  | FORMAT-Help |
@REM
IF "%1" == "/?" GOTO Help
IF "%1" == "b:" GOTO Forbid
IF "%1" == "B:" GOTO Forbid
C:\DOS\FORMAT %1 %2 %3 %4 %5 %6 %7 %8 %9
GOTO End
:Help
ECHO
ECHO  | FORMAT {DD:} {/o}{/v}{/1}{/4}{/8}{/s}{/b}{/n:xx}{/t:yy} |
ECHO  | DD Disk drive label                                     |
ECHO  | /o    : MS DOS 1.x Format                               |
ECHO  | /v    : With name input                                 |
ECHO  | /1    : One side                                        |
ECHO  | /4    : 360 KB two sides                                |
ECHO  | /8    : 8 Sectors                                       |
ECHO  | /s    : Copy system                                     |
ECHO  | /b    : Leave room for system                           |
ECHO  | /n:xx : Number of sectors/track ——\  together only      |
ECHO  | /t:yy : Number of tracks/page   ——/  use                |
ECHO
GOTO End
:Forbid
ECHO This option is not allowed!
GOTO End
:End
@ECHO on
```

By adding these lines we prevent the formatting of the second drive "B:". Try this by removing all of the disks from the disk drives, just in case something does go wrong. Copy the modified batch file into the directory C:\BAT, and then enter:

FORMAT B:

After that the batch file will end with the message:

This option is not allowed !

Now you can change both lines so that the batch file asks for disk drive "C:" instead of disk drive "B:", however don't try parameter "C:".

Explanation

It is important to have the batch file check for both "b:" and "B:", since the IF instruction cannot distinguish between uppercase and lowercase letters. The syntax of MS-DOS commands is not the only problem. The following tips demonstrate other kinds of help.

Creating your own help screens

The problem

At times you may forget where the backslash key is located or which option to use to display a directory in short form or by the page. Although we can't give you tips on remembering everything you may forget, we can show you how to make your own help screens.

The solution

Make a batch named HELP.BAT, that will display on the screen all of the important information and tips you need. The following example will also show you how to display more than one page on the screen so that you can read it at your own pace. For our example you will need the three files HELP.BAT, HELP1.TXT and HELP2.TXT. Let's start with the batch file HELP.BAT.

```
@REM HELP.BAT
@REM
@REM   ┌─────────────────┐
@REM   │ MS-DOS Information │
@REM   └─────────────────┘
@ECHO OFF
CLS
COPY >NUL C:\BAT\HELP1.TXT CON
PAUSE
CLS
COPY >NUL C:\BAT\HELP2.TXT CON
PAUSE
CLS
```

The two files that contain the information are next. Put them in the directory C:\BAT that is specified in the HELP.BAT file. Use no more than 22 lines, including the frame lines for each help screen.

```
                    Help for MS-DOS
     PIPE       ALT+124   |
     Backslash  ALT+92    \
     To reroute use < and > or >>
         .

         .
         .
```

```
                    The best batch files
     WHERFILE.BAT   Searches entire hard disk for files
     DOALL.BAS      Applies a command to all files on the hard disk
     DO.BAT         Applies a command to all files in the directory
     ASCII.BAT      Displays an ASCII-chart
     ASK.COM        Let's you ask questions about ERRORLEVEL
     HELP.BAT       Displays information that will help
     WHEREDIR.BAT   Looks for a subdirectory
     FINDALL.BAT    Looks for specific file, displays in
                    ALLDAT.DAT
     FINDMORE.BAT   Filters through a file list for a criterion
     PW.BAT         Blocks the computer from use by strangers
     BOLD.BAT       Switches the screen to bold-faced type
     NORMAL.BAT     Switches to normal type
     INVERT.BAT     Switches to inverted character representation
```

Explanation

Avoid displaying too many lines on the screen at once, because some lines might scroll off the screen. Use the PAUSE command which must wait for a key press before the COPY command will be able to display the next help screen.

Remember to also use "ECHO off" to stop any further display of the command lines. To prevent the closing message, "1 file(s) copied", the COPY command can be redirected to the NUL device with ">NUL". This device hides all of the data. It is interesting that the device CON represents different "genuine" devices depending on the direction of the data. With input it represents the keyboard and with output it represents the screen. This is useful when you are copying onto CON (onto the screen).

You might be wondering why we copy two text files on the screen instead of using ECHO to display the lines. We do this because certain characters are forbidden in batch files ("<", ">", "|"). So you can't use ECHO to display them.

Since we want to put these characters on the screen, we must write them in a file and copy the file onto the screen.

The ASCII chart at the press of a key

The problem

Have you ever wanted to enter a special character but couldn't remember the proper ASCII code? If you knew the ASCII code you could use the numeric keypad and the <Alt> key to enter it. You can use the following tip to display the ASCII character set on the screen.

The solution

The solution is simple: We create an ASCII chart and use a batch file to copy it to the screen. We could enter the chart by hand, but it's a lot easier to create it with a simple BASIC program. The following BASIC program creates a chart named ASCII.TXT in the directory C:\BAT:

```
5 REM ASCII_CHT.BAS
10 REM Create an ASCII-chart!
12 OPEN "C:\BAT\ASCII.TXT" FOR OUTPUT AS #1
20 FOR i = 32 TO 255 STEP 12
30 FOR j = 0 TO 11
40 IF i + j < 99 THEN PRINT #1, " ";
45 IF i + j < 256 THEN PRINT #1, i + j; CHR$(i + j);
50 NEXT j: PRINT #1,
60 NEXT i
70 CLOSE #1
80 END
```

We still need a small batch file to copy the ASCII chart to the screen. Here is what the batch file ASCII.BAT looks like:

The ASCII chart at the press of a key

```
@REM
@REM   Display ASCII-chart on the screen
@REM
@ECHO off
CLS
COPY >NUL C:\BAT\ASCII.TXT CON
@ECHO on
```

Call this batch file and the following will be displayed on the screen:

```
32      33 !   34 "   35 #   36 $   37 %   38 &   39 '   40 (   41 )   42 *   43 +
44 ,    45 -   46 .   47 /   48 0   49 1   50 2   51 3   52 4   53 5   54 6   55 7
56 8    57 9   58 :   59 ;   60 <   61 =   62 >   63 ?   64 @   65 A   66 B   67 C
68 D    69 E   70 F   71 G   72 H   73 I   74 J   75 K   76 L   77 M   78 N   79 O
80 P    81 Q   82 R   83 S   84 T   85 U   86 V   87 W   88 X   89 Y   90 Z   91 [
92 \    93 ]   94 ^   95 _   96 `   97 a   98 b   99 c  100 d  101 e  102 f  103 g
104 h  105 i  106 j  107 k  108 l  109 m  110 n  111 o  112 p  113 q  114 r  115 s
116 t  117 u  118 v  119 w  120 x  121 y  122 z  123 {  124 |  125 }  126 ~  127 ⌂
128 Ç  129 ü  130 é  131 â  132 ä  133 à  134 å  135 ç  136 ê  137 ë  138 è  139 ï
140 î  141 ì  142 Ä  143 Å  144 É  145 æ  146 Æ  147 ô  148 ö  149 ò  150 û  151 ù
152 ÿ  153 Ö  154 Ü  155 ¢  156 £  157 ¥  158 ₧  159 ƒ  160 á  161 í  162 ó  163 ú
164 ñ  165 Ñ  166 ª  167 º  168 ¿  169 ⌐  170 ¬  171 ½  172 ¼  173 ¡  174 «  175 »
176 ░  177 ▒  178 ▓  179 │  180 ┤  181 ╡  182 ╢  183 ╖  184 ╕  185 ╣  186 ║  187 ╗
188 ╝  189 ╜  190 ╛  191 ┐  192 └  193 ┴  194 ┬  195 ├  196 ─  197 ┼  198 ╞  199 ╟
200 ╚  201 ╔  202 ╩  203 ╦  204 ╠  205 ═  206 ╬  207 ╧  208 ╨  209 ╤  210 ╥  211 ╙
212 ╘  213 ╒  214 ╓  215 ╫  216 ╪  217 ┘  218 ┌  219 █  220 ▄  221 ▌  222 ▐  223 ▀
224 α  225 β  226 Γ  227 π  228 Σ  229 σ  230 µ  231 τ  232 Φ  233 Θ  234 Ω  235 δ
236 ∞  237 ø  238 ∈  239 ∩  240 ≡  241 ±  242 ≥  243 ≤  244 ⌠  245 ⌡  246 ÷  247 ≈
248 °  249 •  250 ·  251 √  252 ⁿ  253 ²  254 ■  255
C:\BAT>
```

Fig 3: The ASCII Chart

As you can see, it would have taken a lot more time to enter the chart by hand than it took to enter this short BASIC program.

Explanation

It is important to use "ECHO off" to stop further display of the command lines and suppress the closing message "1 file(s) copied" by redirecting the COPY command with ">NUL".

45

Displaying files and directories

The most frequently used DOS command is DIR, which is usually not used to its full advantage. In this chapter we will show you what DIR is capable of and a few tricks to use with DIR.

Optimum use of the DIR command

The problem

Simply entering DIR is sufficient for floppy diskettes, but not for hard disks that contain numerous files. There are many options the DIR command has that will help you manage large directories.

The solution

The following chart demonstrates some applications of the DIR command. We assume that C:\ is the current directory:

Displaying files and directories

Command	Displays
DIR A:\	The contents of the main directory of drive A.
DIR A:	The contents of the current directory of drive A.
DIR TEXTS	The contents directory "Texts" (if existing).
DIR *.EXE	All files in the current directory with the ending .EXE.
DIR F*.*	All files and directories (no contents) of the current directory beginning with F.
DIR \	The main directory of the current drive.
DIR ..	The next highest directory (if existing).
DIR /P	All files and directories by page (when the screen is full, MS-DOS will wait for you to press a key before continuing).
DIR /W	All files and directories in wide form (5 columns next to each other).

Explanation

The given options represent only the basic options. You can also combine most of them. For example you could use:

```
DIR A:\*.EXE /p
```

to look at all the files with the extension .EXE in the main directory of drive A one page at a time.

Sorted directories

The problem

Usually MS-DOS determines the order of files being displayed on the screen. This depends on the order in which you created the files. There will probably be times when you would like to rearrange the order of these files.

The solution

You can use the MS-DOS SORT command to sort information. This information can be taken from the keyboard, from a file or from another MS-DOS command (e.g. DIR). To use the last option, enter the pipe symbol "|" between the commands DIR and SORT. International keyboard users can enter the pipe symbol with the numeric keypad using <Alt> + <124>. The following command line displays the current directory sorted alphabetically:

```
DIR | SORT
```

However, the directory will not be displayed in the usual way. The line that ordinarily is displayed last and specifies the number of files and directories, is now the first line. In the course of this chapter we will show you an easier way to sort directories.

Explanation

The SORT command receives the data from the DIR command and sorts every line before displaying it on the screen. The last line has blank spaces at the beginning, which SORT places at the beginning of the display.

Displaying files and directories

> # Displaying directories that are correctly sorted

The problem

If you output a directory that has been sorted, all of the lines will be sorted. This will also sort lines that are message lines and not directory entries.

The solution

Here are some batch files that will sort a directory for various criteria. We also make use of the FIND command. You can use FIND to search for certain contents and then display only those lines with these particular contents or suppress the lines.

In this way you can, for example, filter out the lines with drive and path specifications as well as the line with the number of files.

Tip: The following batch files have some very long lines that are represented as two lines in this book. They must be entered as one line in order for the batch file to operate correctly. Only start a new line if it begins with the character "@". If you are using a version of DOS below 3.3, don't use the @ sign in your batch files. Place an ECHO OFF command as the first line in your batch file to suppress the output.

Sorting files only alphabetically

The following batch file displays only the files in the current directory, sorting by name (there are 12 spaces before the 0 in the last line of the batch file, the last two lines must be entered as one line):

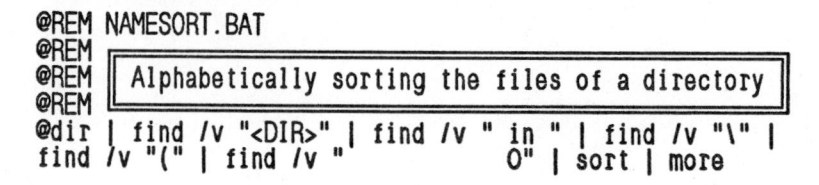

```
@REM  NAMESORT.BAT
@REM
@REM  | Alphabetically sorting the files of a directory |
@REM
@dir | find /v "<DIR>" | find /v " in " | find /v "\" |
find /v "(" | find /v "            0" | sort | more
```

Sorting files only by extension

The following batch sorts files by their extension, (there are 12 spaces before the 0 in the last line of the batch file, the last two lines must be entered as one line):

```
@REM EXTSORT.BAT
@REM
@REM   Files sorted by extension
@REM
@dir | find /v "<DIR>" | find /v " in " | find /v "\" |
find /v "(" | find /v "            0" | sort /+10 | more
```

Sorting files only by size of file

The following batch sorts files by size:

```
@REM SIZESORT.BAT
@REM
@REM   Table of contents only files sorted by size
@REM
@dir | find /v "<DIR>" | find /v " in " | find /v "\" |
find /v "(" | find /v "            0" | sort /+13 | more
```

The following is an example of the screen display of the SIZESORT.BAT file.

```
ASK      COM        9   1-16-90   9:47a
ASK      DEB       70   1-16-90   9:47a
REDIRECT BAT      121   1-16-90   9:20a
HELP     BAT      189   1-16-90  11:20a
HELP     BAK      190   1-16-90  11:19a
DISPASCI BAK      230   1-16-90  10:27a
DISPASCI BAT      230   1-16-90  12:31p
EXESORT  BAK      250   1-16-90  10:28a
EXESORT  BAT      271   1-16-90  12:41p
DAYSORT  BAT      276   1-16-90  10:30a
NAMESORT BAK      289   1-16-90  10:28a
ALPHADIR BAT      291   1-16-90  10:31a
SETPRMPT BAT      293   1-15-90   4:35p
ASCII_CH BAS      295   1-16-90  10:26a
SIZESORT BAK      299   1-16-90  10:29a
TIMESORT BAT      299   1-16-90  10:31a
NAMESORT BAT      307   1-16-90  12:38p
SIZESORT BAT      320   1-16-90  12:42p
NUMBYTE  BAS      359   1-16-90  10:32a
ASKONE   BAT      386   1-16-90   9:57a
WHEREDIR BAT      416   1-16-90  10:33a
WHEREFLE BAT      435   1-16-90  10:34a
-- More --
```

Fig. 4:   *Files sorted by size*

Sorting files only by date

The following batch file sorts files by the day they were created. Unfortunately it is not possible for a complete sorting by date. To do that the date would have to be output in the year-month-day format (remember that the last two lines must be entered as one line):

```
@REM DAYSORT.BAT
@REM
@REM  | Directory - files sorted by day              |
@REM
@dir | find /v "<DIR>" | find /v " in " | find /v "\" |
find /v "(" | find /v "         0" | sort /+24 | more
```

You can sort by month just as easily by replacing the "24" with "27". You can sort by year with "30".

Sorting files only by the date of creation

The following batch file sorts files by the time of creation. Unlike date, it is no problem to have a complete sorting by time, because the time is output in the hours:minutes format (remember that the last two lines must be entered as one line).

```
@REM TIMESORT.BAT
@REM
@REM  | Directory  - only files sorted by time       |
@REM
@dir | find /v "<DIR>" | find /v " in " | find /v "\" |
find /v "(" | find /v "         0" | sort /+35 | more
```

Displaying only alphabetically sorted directories

The following batch file displays only subdirectories, but in alphabetical order. The characters "." and ".." are also displayed because they stand for the current and higher directories (remember that the last two lines must be entered as one line):

```
@REM ALPHADIR.BAT
@REM
@REM  | Directory - only directories alphabetically  |
@REM
@dir | find "<DIR>" | find /v " in " | find /v "\" |
find /v "(" | find /v "         0" | sort | more
```

Explanation

FIND /v "<DIR>" Makes sure that all of the directories are not displayed.

FIND /v "in" Causes the line "Volume in Drive" not to be displayed.

In MS-DOS 4.0 there is an additional line that gives information about the "Volume Serial Number". To remove this line from the sorted directory replace "I FIND /v " in the batch files with "I FIND /v "Volume".

FIND /v "\" This command removes the line containing the name of the directory.

FIND /v "(" This command removes the line containing the number of files and directories.

FIND /v "0" When MS-DOS transmits information from the DIR command, through the FIND and SORT commands, to the MORE command, it sets up temporary files. These files are then erased at the conclusion. You may find these temporary files in a directory. The following is an example of what these files might look like:

```
12123B04        0   5-06-89   6:18p
12123B09        0   5-06-89   6:18p
```

Since there aren't any extensions and they contain 0 bytes at the time of the DIR command, the DIR command removes the temporary files.

SORT Takes care of the sorting process. By entering /+XXX you indicate that sorting should begin after the XXXth character.

MORE This command displays one screen then waits for you to press a key before displaying more.

You might think that you could, instead of using MORE, add a "/P" to the DIR command to get a page by page display of the information on your screen. It won't work. Instead of a page by page display, you may have to (depending on the length of the directory) press a key several times and then all of the results will flash by the screen. The line "Press any key when ready" would be sorted in the output directory! MS-DOS won't pass the information to the first FIND command until the DIR command has displayed all of the information.

Displaying files and directories

> # How many bytes are in the directory?

The problem

Have you ever wondered how much room a particular group of files takes up on your disk or hard disk? This is vital when you want to copy all of the files on a directory from your hard disk onto a floppy diskette, since you need to know if there is enough room on the diskette. Or again, you might want to know how many disks you will need for a BACKUP.

The solution

Simply redirect directory display to a file and use a word processor that computes in columns. The following example uses MS-WORD 5.0:

1. Redirect the directory to a file named:

    DIR >DIR.TXT

2. Start WORD and load the file you have just created. Remove the line DIR.TXT in the listing, because you will erase this file afterwards. It should not be counted along with the other files.

3. Set the cursor to the last digit of the file size in the first file and press <Shift>+<F6> to select the column selection.

4. Move the cursor down and to the left to mark all of the digits of the file sizes.

5. After marking all of the file sizes, press <F2> to add up the marked numbers.

6. You will find the result of the addition in the scrap. So you can simply insert it anywhere in the text with WORD's Insert command.

We have written a small BASIC program NUMBYTE.BAS, for people who don't own a word processor, that can sum columns of numbers. This program reads the directory from the file DIR.TXT and calculates the sum of the file sizes:

How many bytes are in the directory?

```
5 REM NUMBYTE.BAS
10 REM This program determines the size of the files stored
15 REM in DIR.TXT  Use DIR >DIR.TXT to create the file
20 CLS
30 NUMBYTE = 0
40 OPEN "dir.txt" FOR INPUT AS #1
50 WHILE NOT EOF(1)
60 LINE INPUT #1,FILE$
70 NUMBYTE = NUMBYTE + VAL (MID$(FILE$,13,9))
80 PRINT ".";
90 WEND
100 CLOSE #1
110 PRINT
120 PRINT "Size of the files on disk",NUMBYTE
130 END
```

Explanation

The program opens the file DIR.TXT, that you created by redirecting the directory display. The file has to be in the same directory as the BASIC program. The program reads the file line for line until the file ends and takes the part from each line that contains the file size. It also transforms this string into a number and adds them up. At the end the file closes and the program displays the result.

Tip: The specifications of the DIR command indicate the size of the file but not the room that the file takes up on the disk This depends on the minimum amount of storage MS-DOS has for a file. For a diskette there are 1024 bytes, for a PC-XT hard disk there are 2048 bytes and for a PC-AT there are 4096 bytes available.

You can easily determine this by copying the file AUTOEXEC.BAT to an empty disk. If you use DIR to view the size of a file it will be between 50 and 500 bytes. If you call the command CHKDSK for the drive the following line will display:

```
1024 bytes in 1 user file(s)
```

To determine the amount of space used in the files, round off the file size to 1024 bytes per disk, either 2048 or 4096 bytes per hard disk depending on the type of hard disk you have. Since this is really a BASIC problem we won't discuss this further.

Displaying directory structure

The problem

If you call the MS-DOS TREE command (up to and including version 3.3) all directories and subdirectories will be displayed. However, the display won't be very clear because there will be a lot of blank lines between the directory names. Early versions of DOS may not display the Path:, so the following trick will not work with these versions.

The solution

The TREE command displays all of the existing subdirectories. Since it doesn't display them in a clear, readable form, we will show you a couple of tricks that will help improve the display:

Combine the command with MORE and you will be able to view the display at your own pace.

```
TREE | MORE
```

However, you still don't have very much information on the screen, since there are so many blank lines. It would be better if you could only have the main information displayed on the screen.

On the left border of the screen you will see the word "Path". Instead of entering TREE I MORE enter the following line:

```
TREE | FIND "Path" | MORE
```

Tip: Make sure the words in quotation marks are written in uppercase or in lowercase letters!

Now you will only receive one line for each subdirectory, which gives you more information on the screen.

Explanation

If you look closely at the screen display of TREE you will see that the important information always follows "Path:". That is why we filter this information with the command FIND and remove the many unnecessary blank lines. If your version of TREE does not display the Path:, this trick will not work. Later version of DOS have an updated and much improved TREE command.

Searching for subdirectories

The problem

It's easy to lose track of where a subdirectory is located on the hard disk. You might have to look in a lot of directories before finding the right one. However, something can be done to fix this.

The solution

The TREE command displays all of the directories, so you can search for the desired subdirectory at the same time. The following batch WHEREDIR.BAT takes care of that for you (this batch file may not work on any versions of DOS before 3.2):

```
@REM WHEREDIR.BAT
@REM
@REM    Batch file for finding a subdirectory
@REM
@ECHO off
IF "%1" == "" GOTO Error
TREE | FIND "Path:" | FIND "%1" | MORE
GOTO End
:Error
ECHO Searches directories and indicates the subdirectories
ECHO Call: Directory name (without wild cards)
:End
@ECHO on
```

Displaying files and directories

Points to remember

1. Use capital letters for the directory you are looking for.

2. You don't need to specify the entire directory name, you can use part of the name, although you could get other directories as well. For example, "TE" would get you:

   Path: \TEXTS
   Path: \TEMP

3. When you find and display a directory all of the existing subdirectories will also be displayed.

4. The batch for using TREE works for most MS-DOS versions up to and including MS-DOS 3.3. Using TREE with any of the higher versions of MS-DOS would not produce the same results. For a similar solution that applies to higher versions of MS-DOS, check the chapter entitled "Searching for files".

Explanation

TREE displays each subdirectory with the complete path. You can search this output for a desired name. If a directory has subdirectories they will contain the names of all higher directories. This is also the reason why all of the existing subdirectories are displayed.

All file names in alphabetical order

The problem

You can use TREE to output an overview of all the directories of your hard disk. What if you could output all of the files sorted in alphabetical order, regardless of which subdirectory the files are in?

The solution

If you add the parameter /f after TREE, MS-DOS version 3.1 and above, will display all of the files as well. You can filter these and sort them. The following line displays all files with extensions onto the screen a page at a time:

    TREE /F | FIND "." | SORT /+19 | MORE

You could redirect the screen display into a file or print it on a printer. The following line stores this information in the file ALLDAT.TXT on drive A:

    TREE /F | FIND "." | SORT /+19 > A:ALLDAT.TXT

Explanation

To distinguish files from the rest of the information of the TREE command we have to make a compromise. We use the identifying mark "." to separate the filename from the extension. This means that only files with an extension will appear in the sorted list.

The first file of a subdirectory will be displayed with the prefix "File(s)". The following is an example of what part of the screen display would look like:

    File(s)   COMMAND .COM
                 AUTOEXEC.BAT

To prevent the prefix "File(s)" from being sorted and to keep all of the filenames that should be sorted on the right, we don't start sorting until the 19th character (SORT /+19).

Tip: TREE does not display the path names for the files. To display the path name along with the files refer to the chapter on "Sorting files with the correct path specification".

Searching files

Searching for files in all of the directories

The problem

Have you ever searched the entire hard disk for a file and forgotten which directory contained it?

The solution

The following batch file WHERFILE.BAT will search the entire current drive including all subdirectories for filenames, directory names and/or partial names. You must enter the name in capital letters. If you are using a version of DOS below 3.3, don't use the @ sign in your batch files.

```
@REM WHERFILE.BAT
@REM
@REM      Batch file for searching the current drive for a file
@REM
@ECHO off
IF "%1" == "" GOTO Syntax
CHKDSK /v | FIND "%1" | MORE
GOTO End
:Syntax
ECHO Searches for a file in all directories of the current
ECHO drive
ECHO Call: Give file name or partial name
ECHO (CAPITAL LETTERS)
:End
@ECHO ON
```

Searching files

To search for the file BOOK.TXT, enter the filename in uppercase letters. To trace all files beginning with BO, enter \BO. Then enter .TXT to find all files with the ending .TXT. Use CHKDSK /v to find the correct spelling of the file you are looking for.

Explanation

The CHKDSK command checks all files on a disk drive. Enter the parameter /v to have CHKDSK display the file with its complete path. You can also use this with FIND to display certain paths.

Searching files for specific text

The problem

After writing a document and saving it on the hard disk, you forget the filename. So now, you can't find the document. You only remember that the document in the TEXT directory and that a certain term was used in the document.

The solution

The following batch file searches either all the files of a directory or those files you select for a specified text. Enter a filename as your first parameter (wild cards are allowed) and the text, for which you are looking as your second parameter, without quotation marks. You can expand the first parameter by a path specification if you wish. Here are some examples of the calls:

```
FINDTEXT *.TXT invitation
FINDTEXT C:\TEXTS\*.* invitation
```

You must correctly spell the text you are looking for (uppercase or lowercase letters). If you are using a version of DOS below 3.3, don't use the @ sign in your batch files.

Searching files for specific text

```
@REM SRCHFILE.BAT
@REM
@REM   | Batch file for searching files for contents |
@REM
@ECHO off
IF "%1" == "" GOTO Syntax
IF "%2" == "" GOTO Syntax
FOR %%a in (%1) do find "%2" %%a
GOTO End
:Syntax
ECHO Searches for contents in all files in the current
ECHO drive
ECHO Call: File name  Text (File names can contain
ECHO wild cards)
:End
@ECHO ON
```

Unfortunately you cannot use PAUSE or MORE to stop the screen display, because MS-DOS no longer accepts these commands in the FIND line. If this bothers you, here is a slightly modified version that is, however, a little slower:

```
@REM SCHFILE2.BAT
@REM
@REM   | Batch for searching files for contents |
@REM
@ECHO off
IF "%1" == "" GOTO Syntax
IF "%2" == "" GOTO Syntax
ECHO >FIND.TXT ------ The result of the search ------
FOR %%a in (%1) do find >>FIND.TXT "%2" %%a
GOTO End
:Syntax
ECHO Searches for contents in all files in the current
ECHO drive
ECHO Call: File name Text (File names can also contain
ECHO            wild cards)
:End
TYPE FIND.TXT | MORE
@ECHO ON
```

Explanation

After the program checks whether or not both parameters have been entered, the FOR line determines which files could contain the text. These files are passed, with the text in question, to the FIND command. The FIND command searches the file and displays the passage containing the appropriate text.

Searching files

Since you can't stop the screen display, the second batch file uses a trick to display the information in a form that is understandable: It writes a headline in a new file and uses ">>FIND.TXT" to redirect each new message from FIND to this file. At the end of the batch file the new file is displayed a page at a time.

If you want to search all files on the hard disk for a text, then refer to "Using commands on all of the files of a drive" in the next chapter.

Working with multiple files

Using commands on all of the files of a disk drive

The problem

Most MS-DOS commands only work on files that are in the current directory. If you want a command to work on files in all of the subdirectories of a disk, MS-DOS can't help you. However, there are times when it would be convenient if you could, for example, remove all of the temporary files with the ending .TMP from the hard disk or search through all text files on the hard disk for a certain term.

The solution

We have developed a solution for this problem that can be used on most MS-DOS commands and on the files you choose. The solution is made up of two parts:

1. A batch file that finds all the appropriate filenames and writes them in a file.

2. A small BASIC program that develops the appropriate command lines, for MS-DOS, from the filenames and writes the command lines into a new batch file. This newly created batch file automatically solves the problem.

The batch file FINDALL.BAT

Let's begin with the batch file. Save the batch file with the name FINDALL.BAT and keep it in the same directory as the accompanying BASIC program or in a directory in your current path. We recommend that you copy the batch file to the directory C:\BAT of your hard drive and expand the PATH statement in your

Working with multiple files

AUTOEXEC.BAT file to include this directory. The batch file would then look like the following, (if you are using a version of DOS below 3.3, don't use the @ sign in your batch files):

```
@REM FINDALL.BAT
@REM
@REM   Batch file for listing the appropriate files on a disk
@REM
@ECHO off
IF "%1" == "" GOTO Syntax
CHKDSK /v | FIND "\" | FIND /v "Directory" | FIND "%1" >ALLDAT.DAT
GOTO End
:Syntax
ECHO Outputs the appropriate files on the disk drive onto file
ECHO Call: File name (Partial names allowed/Capital letters)
:End
@ECHO ON
```

When you call the batch file give it a filename or part of one as a parameter. All of the eligible files will then be written to the file ALLDAT.DAT in the current directory. The batch file will need our BASIC program later to complete the processing. Remember to use uppercase letters when entering the file name.

Examples for calling FINDALL.BAT

FINDALL .TMP Finds all temporary files.

FINDALL .BAS Locates all BASIC programs; don't forget to use the period as part of the extension so that FINDALL.BAS will locate only the correct files and not GWBASIC.EXE or BASIC.TXT.

FINDALL COMMAND.COM Locates all existing versions of the command interpreters in all directories.

Tip: FINDALL.BAT finds hidden system files but does not distinguish between files you can write to or files you can only read. This could lead to error messages later when the MS-DOS command doesn't find the file.

The BASIC program DOALL.BAS

The program DOALL.BAS takes care of the next part of the task. We kept it as short as possible to cut down on your typing, if you are using a version of DOS below 3.3, don't use the @ sign in lines 270 and 440 in the following program:

```
5 REM DOALL.BAS
10 REM **********************************************************
20 REM *                      DOALL.BAS                         *
30 REM *   Uses an MS-DOS-command on all selected               *
40 REM *   files of the disk drive!                             *
50 REM **********************************************************
60 REM
70 REM Asks for information
80 CLS : PRINT : PRINT
90 PRINT "Enter a part of the file name in CAPITALS"
95 PRINT "Enter the <.> for extensions, example: .TMP"
100 INPUT "Which files should be processed "; FILE$
110 PRINT "Which command should be used on the files "
115 LINE INPUT COMD$
120 PRINT "If necessary, give another parameter or goal"
125 LINE INPUT PARA$
130 INPUT "Turn on ECHO (Y/N)"; ECHO$
140 REM
150 REM Call batch-file FINDALL to get files
170 COMMAND$ = "FINDALL.BAT " + FILE$
180 PRINT COMMAND$
190 SHELL COMMAND$
200 REM
210 REM Select created file and create command lines
220 LNUMBER = 1
230 OPEN "alldat.dat" FOR INPUT AS #1
240 OPEN "DOALL!!!.BAT" FOR OUTPUT AS #2
250 CLS
260 PRINT "The command file DOALL!!!.BAT contains the following lines:"
270 IF ECHO$="N" OR ECHO$="n" THEN PRINT #2,"@ECHO OFF":PRINT "@ECHO OFF"
300 WHILE NOT EOF(1)
310 INPUT #1, FILE$
330 OUTPUT$ = COMD$ + " " + FILE$ + " " + PARA$
340 PRINT OUTPUT$
350 PRINT #2, OUTPUT$
370 LNUMBER = LNUMBER + 1
380 IF LNUMBER < 20 THEN GOTO 420
390 LNUMBER = 1
400 PRINT "Press any key"
410 WHILE INKEY$ = "": WEND
420 REM
430 WEND
440 IF ECHO$="N" OR ECHO$="n" THEN PRINT #2,"@ECHO ON": PRINT "@ECHO ON"
470 CLOSE #2
480 CLOSE #1
490 PRINT "The batch <DOALL!!!.BAT> executes the command for
495 PRINT "all files."
500 PRINT "Attention: Look at the affected lines
510 PRINT "again for safety reasons!!!"
520 PRINT "Press any key to end this program"
525 WHILE INKEY$ = "": WEND
530 CLS
540 END
```

Working with multiple files

Tip: Remember to enter all filenames in uppercase letters when you work with DOALL.BAS. You can replace the line "540 END" with "540 SYSTEM", if you want to continue working with the command interpreter automatically after the program is finished.

Let's turn to the BASIC program. For our first example we will use an MS-DOS command that doesn't make any changes to the files: DIR. This way, we can show you a completely harmless example of the proper use of the program.

We want to locate all versions of COMMAND.COM on the entire disk (in our case hard disk C) and use DIR to display the accompanying data (Size, date, time).

Tip: If GWBASIC gives you an error message in line 190 and won't accept the SHELL command, you have a very old version, from which you cannot call any operating system functions. We recommend that you replace it as soon as possible with a later version.

Load GWBASIC first and then the program DOALL.BAS. Start it with RUN.

1. It will ask you which files to use the command on. Enter COMMAND.COM.

2. The program will then ask you which command to use on all the appropriate files. Enter DIR.

3. The program will then want to know whether or not to provide parameters after the filenames. Since this won't be necessary for our example, press the <Enter> key.

4. The last thing DOALL will want to know is whether or not it should switch on the display of the command lines to the screen (ECHO) for later work. Enter a Y to view the work of the program.

5. The BASIC program will then call the previously created batch file with the correct data and display the call on the screen. In our example the line reads:

    ```
    FINDALL.BAT COMMAND.COM
    ```

6. After the batch file locates all of the appropriate files the BASIC program will create the proper command line for each file and write them in a new batch file named DOALL!!!.BAT. This unusual name is designed to prevent you from accidentally calling this batch file.

Using commands on all of the files of a disk drive

7. The screen will display all of the command lines page by page, so that you can check whether or not only the desired files have been included.

8. At the end the BASIC program (DOALL.BAS) will display the name of the newly created batch file. It will remind you to look at the command batch file once again when using potentially dangerous commands. Then the program ends. Although the DIR command is completely harmless, we want to look at the results of the BASIC program.

9. Use SYSTEM to leave GWBASIC and load DOALL!!!.BAT into a word processor or use TYPE DOALL!!!.BAT to display the file. The following show the results of our hard disk:

    ```
    DIR C:\COMMAND.COM
    DIR C:\DOS\COMMAND.COM
    DIR C:\ORGDAT\COMMAND.COM
    DIR C:\DOS4\COMMAND.COM
    DIR C:\DOS4D\COMMAND.COM
    ```

    There were five command interpreters on our hard disk.

10. Use DOALL!!! to call the final command batch file. This causes all of the existing command interpreters to display with the file size, date and time.

Tip: Remember, don't type any wild cards when using DOALL.BAS, since it would look for these as characters in the file ALLDAT.DAT. Enter ".TXT" instead of "*.TXT".

Before we show you any more tips on how to use DOALL.BAS, we want to explain how the program works.

Explanation

FINDALL uses the CHKDSK command with the /v parameter to output of all files with their path specifications. The first two FIND commands filter out all additional information (disk drive, capacity, processed directories). The last FIND command filters out the files containing the given term. These lines are then directed to the file ALLDAT.DAT.

The BASIC program DOALL.BAS asks for all necessary parameters. Also, the MS-DOS command (Comd$) and a possible parameter (Para$) are entered by means of LINE INPUT so that you can also enter quotation marks. This is sometimes required, for example, as with the FIND command.

Next, we use the SHELL command to call the batch file FINDALL.BAT with the file name you are looking for. The results of the batch file will be in the file ALLDAT.DAT, that will open for reading while the file DOALL!!!.BAT will be opened to output the subsequent command lines. If the ECHO is OFF (display of the command lines of the batch file on the screen), then the command "@ECHO OFF" will be written in the file first. The character "@" prevents this line from displaying on the screen.

The program then reads the file ALLDAT.DAT, line for line. The output line consists of the command, the line that has been read, together with the path and the optional parameter. This new command line is written in the file and displayed on the screen to be checked. Every 20 lines the screen stops and waits for the press of a key so that you can check the lines on the screen at your own pace.

If you write "@ECHO OFF" in the file it will end with "@ECHO ON". The program ends with an important message.

Selecting files with multiple criteria

The problem

While FINDALL is sufficient when it comes to selecting files, sometimes one selection criterion is not enough. For example, you might need to search for all files whose filename begins with "B" and has the ending ".TXT".

The solution

There is a very simple solution for this problem. Call DOALL.BAS with the first criterion and filter out the files with another batch file for the other criteria. The new batch FINDMORE.BAT reads as follows:

Selecting files with multiple criteria

```
@REM FINDMORE.BAT
@REM
@REM  Batch file for multiple criteria selection
@REM
@ECHO off
IF "%1" == "" GOTO Syntax
IF EXIST ALLFILE.OLD DEL ALLFILE.OLD
RENAME ALLDAT.DAT ALLFILE.OLD
FIND <ALLFILE.OLD >ALLDAT.DAT "%1"
GOTO End
:Syntax
ECHO Filters certain files from a file list
ECHO Call: selection criterion
:End
@ECHO ON
```

Enter the batch file with the name FINDMORE.BAT and save it. Store it in the directory C:\BAT or in the directory that contains the BASIC program DOALL.BAS.

This batch file won't do us too much good if we can't call it. For that reason we must make a change on our BASIC program. Enter the following lines in the BASIC program:

```
192 INPUT "Another selection criterion or return";Select$
194 IF Select$ = "" THEN 200
196 COMMAND$ = "FINDMORE.BAT " + Select$
197 SHELL COMMAND$
198 GOTO 192
```

Try out these new options by looking for all files with filenames beginning with "B" and having extension ".BAK". Start up DOALL.BAS and enter:

```
Enter a part of the file name in CAPITALS
Enter the <.> for extensions, example .TMP
Which files should be processed ? \B
Which command should be used on the files
DIR
If necessary give another parameter
.BAK
Turn on ECHO (Y/N)? Y
```

Subsequently our batch file will contain command lines for all files with filenames that start with "B" and have the extension ".BAK".

71

Working with multiple files

Explanation

The batch file FINDMORE.BAT uses "IF EXIST" to check whether or not the file ALLFILE.OLD exists and if so, erases it. Then the file ALLDAT.DAT, which has all of the filenames selected up until now, is renamed ALLFILE.OLD. The FIND command is then called in such a way that it reads its information from the old file, checks all the lines for the given criterion and writes the appropriate lines in the new file ALLDAT.DAT.

The BASIC program asks in the newly inserted command lines, 192-198, whether another criterion for the files should be given. If nothing else is entered the program will continue at line 2000, just like the original version, and will create the command file. Otherwise it will call the batch file FINDMORE with the new selection criterion, create a new file list and then ask whether another criterion for the files should be given.

Perhaps you are wondering why we entered "\B" instead of "B" for the filename. This guarantees that the letter will be at the beginning of the filename and not in the middle of the word.

Searching the entire hard disk

The problem

Have you ever searched for a file on your hard disk, where you only knew one term from the contents? You may have used the batch file from our tip "Searching files for contents". While this tip is handy, it only searches all the files in a given directory. You would have to use this batch file to search through all of the directories of the hard disk, one after the other. DOALL.BAS makes it easy to search all of the directories of the hard disk.

The solution

To solve this problem you need DOALL.BAS and FINDALL.BAT from the previous tip. Let's say you want to search all of the text files on the hard disk for the term "WORD5". Start DOALL.BAS and enter the following:

72

Searching the entire hard disk

```
Enter a part of the file name in CAPITALS
Enter the <.> for extensions, example .TMP
Which files should be processed ?   TXT
Which command should be used on the files
FIND "WORD5"
If necessary give another parameter
.BAK
Turn on ECHO (Y/N)? Y
Other selection criterion:
```

After creating the batch file, call DOALL!!! and all of the searched files will be displayed. If FIND is successful it will display the line containing the correct term.

Explanation

You may be surprised that not only a command but also a parameter is given as "Command". This is necessary because FIND expects the term first and then the file name. We made our program flexible for such cases.

The easy way to search for text

The problem

If your computer is slow, then searching for text could take a long time. If you have to view the screen the whole time it can be very tedious. The following solution is a lot easier.

The solution

The solution for this problem won't cost you much in time. We simply redirect the screen output to the file FIND.TXT, which we can view later at our leisure. Enter >>FIND.TXT as your parameter description.

    Parameter: >>FIND.TXT

Working with multiple files

After you call the batch file you have created you won't get any more screen output. At the conclusion you can use the following command to view the text:

```
TYPE FIND.TXT | MORE
```

Tip: Before starting DOALL!!!.BAT, erase the existing file FIND.TXT.

Explanation

Unfortunately we cannot redirect the screen output of the entire batch file DOALL!!!.BAT to a file since it would not be valid for the FIND command that you call from the batch file. We also cannot simply redirect the screen output for the FIND command with >FIND.TXT, since each new call of the command would erase the existing file. This would mean that the file would only contain the information from the last call.

By redirecting with ">>" we tell MS-DOS to add the screen output to an existing file, just the right solution for our problem. That is why you must erase the file FIND.TXT when you call the batch file, because the new contents would simply be added to the existing, invalid file contents.

Testing all of the files on the hard disk

The problem

Have you ever had an important file suddenly turn unreadable? With diskettes you can protect yourself by making copies. If MS-DOS can read them correctly for copying, it means you are relatively safe from reading defects. With hard disks, on the other hand, it's not so simple.

The solution

You could copy all of the files or even just selected ones onto the hard disk using the BACKUP command. It is, however, a very slow process. MS-DOS has a device called NUL that "swallows" all incoming data. You can use this device to check your files.

Use the BASIC program DOALL.BAS and select the appropriate files. Use COPY as your command and >NUL as your parameter. Then the program will create a new batch file that will copy all of the appropriate files to the NUL device so that they can be checked for legibility.

Erasing files from the entire hard disk

The problem

There are programs that create files that are not deleted. They are often temporary files with the ending ".TMP". There are also backup copies of files that you will only need for a certain time (".SIK" or ".BAK"). To erase these files, you will have to switch from one directory to the next using the DEL command. With a lot of directories this can be very time consuming.

The solution

Our programs DOALL.BAS and FINDALL.BAS provide an extremely simple, but dangerous solution. For example, to erase all temporary files enter ".TMP" for the file name and enter "DEL" as the command. Then the program will create a batch file that erases all undesirable temporary files.

Caution: This program will output all created command lines onto the screen. Check these command lines very carefully so that you don't erase any important files by mistake. Use the DEL command with caution!

Working with multiple files

Processing a directory with all of its subdirectories

The problem

The tips from this chapter have showed you MS-DOS commands for processing all of the files on the hard disk. However, sometimes you only need to process the files in one directory and its subdirectories.

The solution

The solution is simple. Look at the paths created by FINDALL. Enter the directory as your file name enclosed in backslashes "\". If your directory is C:\TEXTS and it contains several subdirectories, every file will have C:\TEXTS\ as its path specification. Simply use

    \TEXTS\

as your filename. If you need to, use the expanded version of DOALL.BAS with more selection criteria to select certain files within the directory.

Sorting all of the files in the correct path

The problem

Do you still know what kind of files you have on your hard disk? After a long work day with a hard disk you can lose track. You could use CHKDSK /V to view all of the files in all of the directories but there are times when you would rather have an alphabetical list of all the files with their path specifications. This enables you to determine if you have two of the same files on the hard disk.

The solution

The following program, SORTFILE.BAS, provides a solution to this problem:

```
10 REM *************************************************
20 REM *                    SORTFILE.BAS               *
30 REM * Sorts all the files of a disk drive and specifies *
35 REM * the path                                       *
40 REM *                                                *
50 REM *************************************************
60 REM
70 REM Request information
80 CLS : PRINT : PRINT
90 INPUT "Output onto screen or into a file (S/F)"; OUTP$
100 IF OUTP$ = "S" OR OUTP$ = "s" THEN OUTP$ = " | MORE"
110 IF OUTP$ = "F" OR OUTP$ = "f" THEN OUTP$ = " >SORTFILE.DAT"
120 SHELL "FINDALL.BAT " + "\"
130 OPEN "ALLDAT.DAT" FOR INPUT AS #1
135 OPEN "ALLFILE.SRT" FOR OUTPUT AS #2
140 WHILE NOT EOF(1)
145 PRINT ".";
150 INPUT #1, IN$
160 L = LEN(IN$)
170 FOR I = L TO 1 STEP -1
180 IF MID$(IN$, I, 1)="\" THEN FILENAME$=MID$(IN$, I+1, L - I): I = 1
190 NEXT I
200 WHILE LEN(FILENAME$) < 15
210 FILENAME$ = FILENAME$ + " "
220 WEND
230 PRINT #2, FILENAME$ + IN$
240 WEND
250 CLOSE #1
260 CLOSE #2
270 COMMAND$ = "SORT < Allfile.SRT " + OUTP$
280 SHELL COMMAND$
290 IF OUTP$ = ">SORTFILE.DAT" THEN PRINT "Sorted file list: SORTFILE.DAT"
300 END
```

Working with multiple files

```
DJ.DS1              C:\SISB\DATA\DJ.DS1
DOALL!!!.BAT        C:\BAT\DOALL!!!.BAT
DOALL.BAS           C:\BAT\DOALL.BAS
DOALL2.BAS          C:\BAT\DOALL2.BAS
DOMERGE.BAS         C:\BAT\DOMERGE.BAS
DOS.INC             C:\UT\INCLUDE\DOS.INC
DOST&T1.DOC         C:\BOOKS\DOS_PROD\DOST&T1.DOC
DOST&T2.DOC         C:\BOOKS\DOS_PROD\DOST&T2.DOC
DOSVERNO.EXE        C:\SISB\DOSVERNO.EXE
DOW.DS1             C:\SISB\DATA\DOW.DS1
DOWJONES.XTS        C:\UT\XTALK\DOWJONES.XTS
DRIVEA              C:\UT\PAINT\DRIVEA
DSKERR.DBF          C:\PCTOOLS\DSKERR.DBF
DUMP.BAT            C:\DOS\DUMP.BAT
ECH.EXE             C:\UT\BIN\ECH.EXE
EDITCVT.BAK         C:\BOOKS\PC_PRINT\EDITCVT.BAK
EDITCVT.BAS         C:\BOOKS\PC_PRINT\EDITCVT.BAS
EDITCVT.EXE         C:\BOOKS\PC_PRINT\EDITCVT.EXE
EDLIN.COM           C:\DOS\EDLIN.COM
EGABW.OV1           C:\UT\PAINT\EGABW.OV1
EGACLR.OV1          C:\UT\PAINT\EGACLR.OV1
EGAFHDR.INF         C:\GEMAPPS\FONTS\EGAFHDR.INF
EGAFSTR.INF         C:\GEMAPPS\FONTS\EGAFSTR.INF
-- More --
```

Fig. 5:   *All files alphabetically sorted*

User and data protection

If several people have access to your computer, this chapter will provide some useful tips on how to protect your computer and data from interference by outsiders.

Has someone been using my computer?

The problem

Suppose that you don't want anyone to use your computer unless he/she asks for your permission first. You also need to know when someone has used your computer without asking.

The solution

To determine whether anyone has been using your computer without permission, simply store the time and date that the computer was last used. Then you can easily check whether or not someone used the computer.

In order to figure out the time and date your computer was last used, you must redirect this information to a file. Just recording the time and date the computer was last switched on isn't sufficient because you must switch on the computer in order to read this information from the file. So, the file would show the time, at which you switched on the computer in order to check the file, as the last time the computer had been switched on. This means that you need two files: one file that contains the time and date the computer was last switched on and another file to store the time and date you switched on the computer to check the file.

User and data protection

Since you don't want anyone to know about this, the screen shouldn't display any messages that explain the operation. It's also important that the <Enter> key is pressed after calling the MS-DOS commands DATE and TIME, so that these commands can be executed.

To do this, we redirect the <Enter> key, in a file named RETURN, so that it contains the character for the <Enter> key. We need the following to log our computer clock watcher:

1. A directory such as C:\TEMP to store the time and date. You can use a different directory when entering the following commands.

2. The directory BAT to keep the file named RETURN for redirecting the <Enter> key input. You could also choose a different directory for this.

3. The file RETURN, which is easy to create. Enter:

    COPY CON C:\BAT\RETURN

    and press the <Enter> key once. Finish the command with <Ctrl> + <Z> and the <Enter> key. Now the RETURN file contains the value of the <Enter> key.

4. Now enter the three new lines in the AUTOEXEC.BAT file to store the date. These lines copy the existing file, DTIME, into TIME.OLD, write the time in the DTIME file and add the date. The new lines and the associated directories will look like the following, you may have to change the directories for your system:

Tip: The "@" symbol will not work with DOS version 3.2 and below. Instead, "Echo off" must be used. The following lines should be used with Version 3.2 and below:

```
echo off
rem timekeep.bat
copy >NUL c:\temp\dtime c:\temp\dtime.old
time >c:\temp\dtime <c:\bat\return
date >>c:\temp\dtime <c:\bat\return
```

For MS-DOS Version 3.3 and higher:

```
@copy >NUL c:\temp\dtime c:\temp\dtime.old
@time >c:\temp\dtime <c:\bat\return
@date >>c:\temp\dtime <c:\bat\return
```

Tip: If the lines in the AUTOEXEC.BAT seem too conspicuous, write them in a batch file CHKDSK.BAT and then call this file from AUTOEXEC.BAT. Since the batch has the same spelling, everyone will think it's the CHKDSK command.

The first time you call the AUTOEXEC.BAT there will not be a DTIME file. Since we are suppressing the screen output of the COPY command with >NUL, there won't be a visible error message. After making these adjustments you can display the date and time the computer was last used by using the following command:

```
TYPE C:\TEMP\DTIME.OLD
```

Explanation

Using the character "@" (ECHO OFF, in Version 3.2 and below) before the three new command lines in the AUTOEXEC.BAT ensures that these lines won't be displayed on the screen. But the COPY command message, "1 file copied", would appear anyway. This is why we redirect the output of the command to the device NUL, which simply "hides" all the data. So the message isn't displayed.

Next we redirect the output into the TIME file and obtain the input from the RETURN file, which contains the character for the <Enter> key. In this way we outsmart MS-DOS and simulate pressing the <Enter> key. So the user doesn't need to press it.

While redirecting the time into the file with ">C:\TEMP\TIME", we must use ">>" for the second redirection so that the old contents are preserved and the new message is added only to the existing file.

Who was the last person to use my computer?

The problem

Sometimes you want to know not only if your computer has been used but also who has been using it.

User and data protection

The solution

Specify that a person must enter his/her name when using the computer. The time and date must also be entered with the user's name.

To do this we only need a small machine language program and a few lines in the AUTOEXEC.BAT file. Since input isn't possible with the commands in the batch files, the machine language program is needed in order to determine the user's name.

Enter the following lines with an editor, name the file INPUT.DEB. If you use the editor EDLIN, start it with the following:

```
EDLIN INPUT.DEB
```

Press "I" and the <Enter> key to insert lines. Enter the following lines exactly as printed:

```
A
MOV AH,08
INT 21
MOV DL,AL
MOV AH,02
INT 21
CMP AL,0D
JNZ 0100
MOV DL,0A
INT 21
MOV AL,00
MOV AH,4C
INT 21

RCX
18
nINPUT.COM
W
Q
```

Press <Ctrl>+<Z> and "E" to store the file you have created with EDLIN.

To make a machine language program out of this file, call the debugger, DEBUG with the following:

```
DEBUG <Input.deb
```

Who was the last person to use my computer?

After DEBUG has processed this file, you can use the machine language program INPUT.COM, located in the current directory. Copy this into a directory in the current path, for example C:\BAT.

Next we need a few new lines in the AUTOEXEC.BAT to record the name of the last user as well as the date and time. Add the following lines to your AUTOEXEC.BAT file:

Note: "@" cannot be used with DOS version 3.2 and below

```
@ECHO OFF
REM LOGUSER.BAT
BREAK OFF
IF EXIST C:\TEMP\USER.LOG COPY >NIL C:\TEMP\USER.LOG
C:\TEMP\USER.OLD
ECHO Please enter name
INPUT >C:\TEMP\USER.LOG
DATE <C:\BAT\RETURN >>C:\TEMP\USER.LOG
TIME <C:\BAT\RETURN >>C:\TEMP\USER.LOG
BREAK ON
@ECHO ON
```

The next time you start your PC, the following prompt will appear:

```
Please enter name
```

You can enter your name even though the characters will not be displayed on the screen. This is harmless and enables you to use the program to enter passwords that shouldn't appear on the screen. The input name, time and date are stored in the file USER.LOG in the directory C:\TEMP.

To determine who was the last person to use your PC, simply switch on the computer, enter your name and look at the file USER.OLD. All the information will be recorded there.

Explanation

We first check whether or not the file USER.LOG already exists. If it does, we copy it as USER.OLD. Then we output the request "Please enter your name". Next we use the newly created program INPUT.COM.

The machine language program will call characters from the input device (in our example, the keyboard) until the <Enter> key is pressed. Because of the redirection in the call these characters are sent to the file USER.LOG.

User and data protection

The last step is to add the date and time to the file (>>). Once this is done, the desired information is stored.

How long did someone work on my computer?

The problem

If you would also like to know how much time someone spent working on your PC, you will need to do more than record the user's name and starting time. You also need to record the time the computer was switched off.

The solution

The simplest way to do this is to create a batch file named END.BAT and have the user call this file before turning off the computer. This batch file could look like this:

```
@ECHO OFF
REM END.BAT
ECHO >>C:\TEMP\USER.LOG turned off at:
DATE <C:\BAT\RETURN >>C:\TEMP\USER.LOG
TIME <C:\BAT\RETURN >>C:\TEMP\USER.LOG
@ECHO ON
```

Note: If you are using DOS version 3.2 or below, you cannot use the "@" symbol in your batch files.

By using this batch file, you can add to the USER.LOG file, the date and time the PC was switched off.

Perhaps you don't want the user to know that you are recording this information. Simply give the user an important reason to call a program when he/she is finished using the computer.

You could use the program PARK, which secures the hard drive so that any impact will not harm it. Rename PARK.COM (if you have one) to _PARK.COM and create a batch PARK.BAT, which could look like the following:

```
@ECHO OFF
ECHO >>USER.LOG turned off at:
DATE <C:\BAT\RETURN >>USER.LOG
TIME <C:\BAT\RETURN >>USER.LOG
_PARK
@ECHO ON
```

Tip: You may be wondering why we renamed PARK.COM to _PARK.COM. We did this to avoid a continuous loop (the batch file PARK.BAT continuously calling itself instead of calling the COM program.) Also, if C:\DOS is the current directory, the program PARK.COM would be called instead of the batch file.

Simply inform the user that, because of safety reasons, the hard drive has to be secured (parked) and that he/she has to enter "PARK" when finished with the computer. Once this is done, the time that the PC was switched off will automatically be stored in the file USER.OLD.

Explanation

It is important to rename the command PARK to _PARK so that the batch file will be called when "PARK" is entered. By doing this, the date and time are added to the file USER.LOG and the renamed command _PARK is called. The user won't notice anything.

How do you protect your computer while it's in use?

The problem

Suppose that while you are working on your computer you have to leave it for a short time. However, you don't want to switch off your PC. You need a way to prevent someone from using your PC and/or from looking at your data while you're away.

The solution

Before leaving the computer, call a BASIC program that will end only after a certain word has been entered. This type of program could look like this:

```
5 REM PASSWORD.BAS
10 REM PW.BAS
20 PW$ = "msdos"
30 REM
40 REM INPUT
50 CLS
60 FOR I = 1 TO LEN(PW$)
70 N$ = MID$(PW$, I, 1)
100 GOSUB 150
110 IF N$ <> A$ THEN BEEP: GOTO 40 :REM input
120 NEXT I
130 SYSTEM
140 REM
150 REM CHARACTER:
160 A$ = INKEY$
170 IF A$ = "" THEN GOTO 150
180 PRINT ".";
190 RETURN
```

Store the program under the name PW.BAS (password) in the directory C:\BAT. When you start this program the screen will clear and the program will wait for the proper characters to be entered (in this example, "msdos"). A period will appear on the screen for each correct character. Since the entered characters will not be displayed on the screen, no one is able to read the key word.

When all the characters have been properly entered, the program will end. Otherwise there will be a warning sound after the first incorrect character and the characters will have to be re-entered. The easiest way to start the program is to create a batch file named PW.BAT that contains the following:

    @GWBASIC C:\BAT\PW.BAS

Now you can call user protection program by entering PW.

Explanation

This program cannot be stopped by pressing <Ctrl> + <C> because, in GWBASIC, this key combination creates a character with the ASCII value 3, which doesn't immediately stop the program. The only way to stop the program is to press <Ctrl> +<Break>.

Compiling the program with QuickBasic will prevent the program from stopping entirely. Even <Ctrl> +<Break> won't have any effect.

How do you protect your computer from unwanted use?

The problem

Suppose that you want to prevent someone from using your computer without your knowledge.

The solution

To do this, simply add the lines used to call the program PW.BAS to the AUTOEXEC.BAT file. Now the password must be entered at the beginning of the session. You should compile the program so that it can't be stopped by using <Ctrl> + <Break>. However, someone could still use the computer by bringing his/her own MS-DOS boot disk, which doesn't ask for the password.

Explanation

This protective measure is effective only when more than one user has access to the computer. If someone needs to work by his/herself, you would have to reveal the password. So, the password would no longer be useful.

The next tip will show you how to protect data from being changed or examined if other people need to use your computer.

How do you protect data and directories?

The problem

You allow others to use your computer without being able to access all of the data contained on the computer.

User and data protection

The solution

The easiest way to do this is to store the data on only one diskette and then safely lock it away somewhere. However, often this is impractical. For example, this method wouldn't work with large amounts of data contained on a hard disk that must be constantly available. A relatively simple solution is to conceal the data.

MS-DOS uses two hidden files (IBMBIO.COM, IBMDOS.COM or other files, depending on the system.) You cannot work on these files with the regular MS-DOS commands (DIR, COPY, DEL.) However, there isn't an MS-DOS command that can conceal files and then retrieve them.

The following machine language program, HIDE.COM, enables you to hide files and then retrieve them at any time. Since the program is too long to be produced completely trouble free with DEBUG, we are printing it as a BASIC program using DATA statements to make its entry easier.

```
5 REM HIDE.BAS
10 REM Program to produce HIDE.COM
20 RESTORE
30 SUM=0: N=0
40 WHILE N <> -1
50 READ N
60 SUM = SUM + N
70 WEND
80 IF SUM <> 21708 THEN PRINT "Checksum error!!! ";SUM;" instead of 21708": END :REM enter on one line
90 OPEN "hide.com" FOR OUTPUT AS #1
100 RESTORE
110 N = 0
120 WHILE N <> -1
130 READ N
135 IF N = -1 THEN 150
140 PRINT #1,CHR$(N);
150 WEND
160 CLOSE #1
170 PRINT "Everything ok - Program HIDE.COM produced"
180 END
500 DATA   187, 128,   0,  51, 192, 138,   7, 60
510 DATA     0, 116, 123,  67, 138,  39, 128,252
520 DATA    13, 116, 115, 128, 252,  32, 117,  6
530 DATA   254, 200, 116, 106, 235, 237, 139,211
540 DATA    67, 138,  39, 128, 252,  13, 116, 11
550 DATA   128, 252,  32, 116,   6, 254, 200,116
560 DATA    85, 235, 237,  80,  51, 192, 136 , 7
570 DATA    88, 254, 200, 116,  73,  67, 138, 39
580 DATA   128, 252,  13, 116,  65, 128, 252,104
590 DATA   116,  21, 128, 252,  72, 116,  16,128
600 DATA   252, 117, 116,  17, 128, 252,  85,116
```

```
610 DATA    12, 254, 200, 116,  41, 235, 223,185
620 DATA     2,   0, 235,   4, 144, 185,   0 ,0
630 DATA   180,  67, 176,   1, 205,  33, 114,11
640 DATA   180,   9, 186, 198,   1, 205,  33,180
650 DATA    76, 205,  33, 180,   9, 186, 145,  1
660 DATA   205,  33, 180,  76, 205,  33, 180,  9
670 DATA   186, 160,   1, 205,  33, 180,  76,205
680 DATA    33,  69, 114, 114, 111, 114,  32,58
690 DATA    70, 105, 108, 101,  33 , 13,  10,36
700 DATA    83, 121, 110, 116,  97, 120,  58,32
710 DATA    70, 105, 108, 101,  95, 110,  97,109
720 DATA   101,  32,  72,  47,  85,  32,  40,104
730 DATA   105, 100, 101,  47, 117, 110, 104,105
740 DATA   100, 101,  41,  13,  10,  36, 111,107
750 DATA    13, 10, 36, -1
```

After entering the program, store it under the name HIDE.BAS and run it. The machine language program HIDE.COM will be produced in the current directory. This should be copied to a directory in the current path that is easily accessible.

Concealing files

To conceal a file, enter the filename after HIDE by using the character "h" (for hide) as an additional parameter. Try it out by first copying the file COMMAND.COM onto a blank, formatted disk in drive A: and then hiding it:

    HIDE A:\COMMAND.COM h

HIDE.COM answers with "ok". Use DIR to check if the file is still visible. You will see that only the missing space on the disk indicates a hidden file. If there are other visible files on the disk, most likely no one will notice the available storage space.

You can try other MS-DOS commands but you cannot copy, erase or do anything else to the hidden file.

Making files visible

To make the file visible again, enter:

    HIDE A:\COMMAND.COM u

After the message "ok", the file COMMAND.COM will be visible again and you will be able to use MS-DOS commands to copy or delete it.

User and data protection

You can also use HIDE.COM to make the hidden systems files of a boot disk visible. If you still have the formatted disk in the drive, copy the hidden systems files onto this test disk with SYS. Now we'll make these files visible:

Tip: The SYS command causes the hidden MS-DOS files to be copied onto a data diskette.

For PC-DOS   HIDE A:IBMBIO.COM u
               HIDE A:IBMDOS.COM u

For MS-DOS   HIDE A:IO.SYS u
               HIDE A:MSDOS.SYS u

```
C:\BAT>hide a:ibmbio.com u
ok

C:\BAT>hide a:ibmdos.com u
ok

C:\BAT>dir a:

 Volume in drive A has no label
 Directory of A:\

IBMBIO   COM    7820   8-09-85  12:00p
IBMDOS   COM   27760   8-09-85  12:00p
        2 File(s)    325632 bytes free

C:\BAT>hide
Syntax: File_name H/U (hide/unhide)

C:\BAT>hide a:no_file h
Error :File!

C:\BAT>
```

Fig. 6:   Hidden files are now visible

If HIDE.COM doesn't find the given file, the following error message will appear:

   Error:File

You can now look at the once hidden system files by using DIR.

Hiding directories

If you want to protect more than one file from unauthorized access simply place all of the files in a directory and then hide the directory. In contrast to hidden files, you can select a hidden directory and work with its files as long as you know the name of the directory.

Suppose that you are filing all of your private data in the directory C:\PRIVAT. The following command line:

    HIDE C:\PRIVAT h

will hide this directory. You can still select it by entering CD C:\PRIVAT and begin working with the files.

Tip: If you enter the parameter /v, the command CHKDSK will display all the files of a data disk - even the hidden files. The file system in the MS-DOS 4.0 shell also displays visible and hidden files.

Explanation

In every file, MS-DOS stores four attribute bytes along with the other data. These attributes are:

MS-DOS attributes	
Hidden	hidden file
System	system file
Read	Read only file
Archive	files changed since the last backup

You can change two of these attributes with the MS-DOS 3.2 command ATTRIB (Read and Archive). The other attributes can't be changed by MS-DOS commands.

Tip: When you call the program HIDE.COM, it not only changes the attribute Hidden, but all the attributes. In order to avoid this, HIDE would have to first determine the attributes of the given file and then change only the Hidden attribute. Otherwise, the program would be much longer.

User and data protection

How do you protect special files and directory names?

The problem

You don't want your hidden files and directories to be displayed with CHKDSK, and you don't want to make it more difficult to remember filenames.

The solution

To make it harder to input a filename, simply begin the filename with a blank character (<Alt> + <255>). Although this character looks like a space, MS-DOS interprets it as a legitimate character. To create such a file or directory name follow these instructions:

1. Enter <Alt> + <255>; a blank will appear on the screen.

2. Enter the remaining 7 characters and any extensions.

A directory with such a file could look like the following:

```
Volume in drive A has no label
Directory of A:\

COMMAND   COM    26076  11.11.87  12.00
AUTOEXEC  BAT      201  10.05.89  13.55
CONFIG    SYS      116   9.05.89   1.56
TEST               23   6.05.89  19.58
 TEST              23   6.05.89  19.58
```

As you can see, the file TEST is indented by one character; it begins with a blank. Since this could be detected by a user, we'll show you another way to do the same thing. Look at the following directory:

How do you protect special files and directory names?

```
Volume in drive A has no label
Directory of  A:\

COMMAND  COM    26076  11.11.87  12.00
AUTOEXEC BAT      201  10.05.89  13.55
CONFIG   SYS      116   9.05.89   1.56
TEST               23   6.05.89  19.58
TEST               23   6.05.89  19.58
```

As you can see, there are two identical TEST files. This is not a printing error in the book, but rather a clever use of the "blank". The first file is called TEST and the second one is called TEST.<ALT 255>. According to MS-DOS these two filenames are not identical so you are able to have two apparently identical files in one directory.

You can use this technique to prevent access to this file. If you also give the file an invisible extension, it will be almost impossible for someone to enter the filename correctly. Furthermore, anyone who did try to enter the name would be amazed that MS-DOS, in spite of seemingly correct entry, would always answer with the following message (e.g. TYPE or COPY):

```
File not found
```

A completely hidden directory

The problem

It is more difficult to display hidden files with CHKDSK than by displaying them in the DOS 4.0 Shell File System, which significantly limits protection. Even though hidden files can't be copied or erased, they can be displayed with DOS 4.0 Shell File System's VIEW function.

The solution

Create a new directory whose name consists of the blank character <Alt>+<255> and then use the HIDE program to hide it. Since MS-DOS 4.0 will no longer be

User and data protection

able to select or display this directory in the Shell File System, no one can reach these files through the DOS 4.0 Shell File System.

To prevent a <DIR> from displaying the date and time, simply use HIDE to conceal the directory. We will show you how to create and work with this kind of secured directory. Enter the fictitious blank directory by using <Alt>+<255>:

1. A:
2. CD \
3. MD <ALT+255>
4. HIDE <ALT+255> h

The directory is now available even though it is hidden. For example, to copy the file COMMAND.COM from the main directory of drive C: into this directory, use the following procedure:

1. CD <ALT+255>
2. COPY C:\COMMAND.COM A:<ALT+255>

Now the command interpreter is on the diskette in drive A in the hidden blank directory. If you wanted to use CD.. to change it to the main directory of A, using DIR will no longer display anything because this disk contains the hidden blank directory.

Tip: You will find out about more of the special capabilities of MS-DOS 4.0 in the chapter covering this DOS version.

Printer Tips and Tricks

Using MS-DOS it's possible to display a variety of characters per line and set various line spacings. But when compared to other commercial programs, which have many elaborate printing drivers, MS-DOS barely supports the printer. In this chapter we will discuss the available options and will show you how to gain better control of your printer using MS-DOS.

Print 132 or 80 characters per line

The problem

You have probably written programs in which your longer program lines have been divided into two lines when they are printed out. This makes the program more difficult to read. Perhaps the charts you've created, aren't formatted correctly when printed. In these instances it would be helpful if MS-DOS could be used in order to make the printer use smaller print.

The solution

By using the MODE command you can convert the number of characters per line from 80 to 132, if your printer will support a font that is narrow enough to do this. The command for a printer that is connected to the first printer port is as follows:

```
MODE LPT1:132
```

Create a batch file named 132.BAT for this conversion:

Printer Tips and Tricks

Do not use the "@" symbol if you are working with DOS version 3.2 or below.

```
@REM
@REM   Convert the printer to 132 Characters per line
@REM
@ECHO off
MODE >nil LPT1:132
@ECHO on
```

You probably don't want to print all of your text in this print size because it's so small. This is why you must be able to switch back to 80 characters per line. The following line will convert the printed output back to the normal print size:

```
MODE LPT1:80
```

Create a batch file named 80.BAT, which contains this line:

```
@REM
@REM   Convert the printer to 80 characters per line
@REM
@ECHO off
MODE >nil LPT1:80
@ECHO on
```

If you have Multiplan and it is in the directory C:\MP, you can combine calling your spreadsheet and converting the number of characters per line by using the following batch file, MP.BAT (The CALL command only works on DOS versions greater than 3.2, earlier version should use COMMAND /C):

```
@REM
@REM   Batch to call multiplan with 132 chars/line
@REM
@ECHO off
@CALL 132
C:\MP\MP %1 %2 %3 %4 %5
@CALL 80
@ECHO on
```

In order for the new line width to be used, you should increase the width of the print in Multiplan by using PRINT MARGIN BORDER.

Adjusting various line spacings

The problem

In order to fit a large amount of text on one page, there must be more lines on the page in addition to more characters on a line.

The solution

MODE allows you to change not only the number of characters per line but also the line spacings. The standard value is 80 characters per line and 6 lines per inch. You can adjust this at any time with:

```
MODE LPT1:80,6
```

Using the 132 characters per line font allows you to easily fit 8 lines per inch. To do this use the following command:

```
MODE LPT1:132,8
```

Continuous computer paper is 11 inches long, or 27.94 centimeters. Printing text with 132 characters and 8 lines per inch allows you to fit 2.2 times more characters on a sheet of paper, which is helpful for summaries and tables.

Using a second printer port

The problem

Perhaps you have two parallel printers that you would like to use together or maybe your printer isn't working properly and you would like to find out whether the printer or computer is causing the problem. You should check to see if your

Printer Tips and Tricks

computer has two connections for the printer. If it does, the second port can be used in these instances.

The solution

Without knowing how many ports your PC has for external devices, you may buy a printer switch so that you can connect two parallel printers (for example a dot matrix printer and a daisy wheel printer). However, you may have wasted your money if find that your PC already has a second port. So it is important that you check the back of your computer to see if there is another identical jack. If there is, you can connect another printer there. To print on the second printer use LPT2 instead of LPT1.

Even if there is only one port, it may be better to buy a second port than a printer switch. Usually the adapter comes with a clock or an additional serial connection and costs less than a printer switch.

If you think that your printer isn't working properly (i.e., interrupts during printing, doesn't print complete characters, omits characters) and would like to find out whether the printer or the computer is at fault, simply hook up the printer to the second port and perform a test run on LPT2.

If the printer works properly, then something is probably wrong with the LPT1 port. This means that you don't have to have your PC repaired since you can still use the second port, LPT2. If the error appears again, something is probably wrong with the printer.

Easy printer programming

The problem

The MS-DOS MODE command performs two adjustments for you: it sets the number of characters per printed line and the number of lines per inch. Your printer may be capable of doing more, but MS-DOS may not be able to handle the same parameters as your printer. You must send control codes to your printer. However, you may not be able to access most of these characters from your keyboard. Although you can access many of the characters using the <Alt> key and the numeric keypad, many of these key combinations may produce printed results other than the desired results.

The solution

A simple way to send almost any characters to the printer is to enter the characters in a file and then copy the file to the printer. Then the printer interprets the characters as commands.

Since you will create this file only once, we will create the program to do this in GWBASIC. Using the BASIC command CHR$() you can transform every number between 0 and 255 into a character and direct them, with PRINT#, into a file.

Since this book is about tips and tricks with MS-DOS and not BASIC programming, we will only briefly explain the BASIC program. Load GWBASIC and enter the following program. Save it with SAVE PRTDAT.BAT and start it with RUN. Enter BELL.PRT as the filename and after the program ends, leave BASIC with SYSTEM. Now you can copy the control file onto the printer by using the following command:

    COPY BELL.PRT LPT1

Listen for the printer's warning bell.

```
10 REM
20 REM   Program to create printer-escape sequences
30 REM                   PRTDAT.BAS
40 REM
50 INPUT "Please give file name for the data:";FILE$
60 OPEN FILE$ FOR OUTPUT AS #1
70 READ VALUE%
80 IF VALUE% = -1 THEN 200
90 IF VALUE% < 0 OR VALUE% > 255 THEN PRINT "Error!", VALUE%: END
100 PRINT #1,CHR$(VALUE%);
110 GOTO 70
200 CLOSE #1
210 PRINT "File created"
220 END
500 DATA 7,7,7,-1
```

To set up the program for your own printer control files you must enter the correct data in line 500, after "DATA". Refer to the ASCII chart and the escape sequences in your printer manual for the commands. If the data won't fit on one line, you can use a command similar to the following in order to add more lines:

    510 DATA 1,2,3,4,5,-1

Printer Tips and Tricks

It is important that "-1" appear only once and at the end of the line because this number signals to the program the end of the data for the control file.

Now we will create a second control file which will demonstrate how this program is used. This file will be used for a form feed. EPSON compatible printers will need to send the character with the ASCII value for 12. On line 500 of the BASIC program, we enter:

```
500 DATA 12,-1
```

Start the program and enter FF.PRT as the filename (always use the extension PRT with printer control files). Then use the following command line in order to send a form feed onto the printer:

```
COPY FF.PRT LPT1
```

If you look through your printer manual, you will find many other interesting applications. These applications range from setting bold type, underlining, adjusting proportional type and changing tabs to defining new characters. Since our book is about DOS tips and tricks, we will not discuss these printer applications.

You can use a batch file to copy your control files. The following program illustrates sending a form feed to your printer:

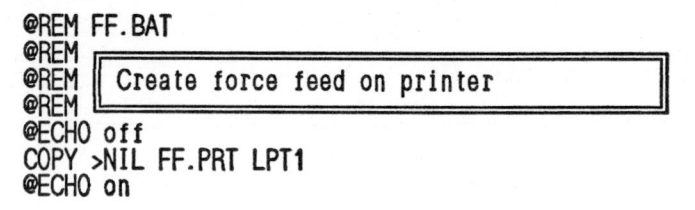

```
@REM FF.BAT
@REM
@REM   Create force feed on printer
@REM
@ECHO off
COPY >NIL FF.PRT LPT1
@ECHO on
```

Does your printer print all the IBM characters?

The problem

Sometimes it is important to know whether your printer is printing all of the IBM characters correctly. This can help you find any defects in your printer.

The solution

Earlier you learned how to create an ASCII chart of all printable characters, from 32 to 255, by pressing a single key. Use the following line to output this chart and check whether all the characters have been printed correctly on your printer.

```
COPY C:\BAT\ASCII.TXT LPT1
```

Screen Modes

MS-DOS allows you to select different screen modes and character display. We'll begin by discussing the most practical modes, which are used by all PC owners. In order to use the following capabilities, you must use a special device driver: ANSI.SYS. You will need the following line in your CONFIG.SYS to load the ANSI.SYS driver when your computer is turned on:

```
DEVICE=C:\DOS\ANSI.SYS
```

If you have installed MS-DOS in another directory, you'll have to enter a different path after the equal sign. If you haven't added ANSI.SYS to your CONFIG.SYS yet and would like to, you must restart your PC with <Ctrl> + <Alt> + <Del> so that this change can take effect.

Using character attributes to emphasize text

The problem

Sometimes you may want to emphasize text on the screen, for example with bold type. You can do this by using special PROMPT command instructions. Make sure your CONFIG.SYS files contains the ANSI.SYS device driver command described above or the following will not work.

The solution

You can change the *screen attributes*, which refers to how the character is represented on the screen, using the PROMPT command. Enter the following line:

Screen Modes

        PROMPT $e[5m

Note: If the square bracket isn't available on your international keyboard, press <Alt> + <91> to produce this character.

Nothing seems to have changed except that the "C:\" has disappeared. Enter a character on the blank line and it will start to blink. Enter DIR and press the <Enter> key. Now you have a blinking directory on the screen. After the command line, the next characters you enter will blink. You can use the following line in order to switch back to the normal screen display:

        PROMPT $e[0m

However, this will only apply to the characters entered after this point. To remove the remaining blinking characters from the screen, use CLS.

Explanation

In order to understand why only certain parts of the screen are affected by the command, you must know how the screen contents are stored for screen display. There is a memory location, representing each screen location, that specifies which character should be displayed. A different memory location specifies how the character should appear on the monitor (normal, blinking, etc.) When a character is displayed on the screen, the value for the character is written in one memory location while the *character attribute* is written in the other memory location. The PROMPT command we gave ensures that all of the subsequent characters in the attribute byte (the memory location for the character attribute) will contain the value for "blink".

These character sequences, called "$e[0m" escape sequences, are initiated by the Esc character so that ANSI.SYS can recognize them as commands. Since the <ESC> key erases the input line, the character sequence "$e is used within the PROMPT command. To experiment with other character attributes, enter:

        PROMPT $e[?m

Note: Choose a value for ? from the following chart.

Value for ?	Result
0	normal
1	bold type
4	underline (color monitors: (color change)
5	blinking
7	inverse video
8	invisible

The solution

You should create batch files for the desired attributes. We'll show you two examples. The first program, BOLD.BAT switches to bold type and the second program, NORMAL.BAT switches back to normal type.

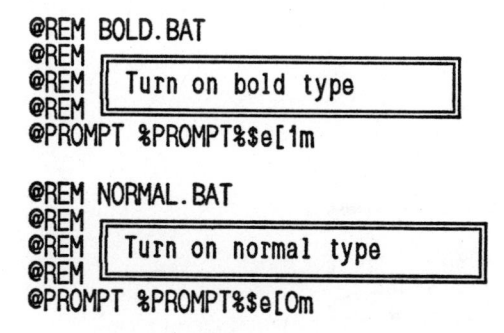

```
@REM  BOLD.BAT
@REM
@REM   | Turn on bold type |
@REM
@PROMPT %PROMPT%$e[1m
```

```
@REM  NORMAL.BAT
@REM
@REM   | Turn on normal type |
@REM
@PROMPT %PROMPT%$e[0m
```

Tip: Both of these batch files will cause problems if you still haven't defined a prompt. Before these batch files are used, the drive letter is the prompt. However, this isn't true after using the batch. So, you can either define a prompt that is useful in the batch file or use the batch file extension, which is described on the following pages.

We have written another program that displays the text in normal and bold type so that you can try both batch files. The CALL command will not work if you are using a version of DOS below 3.3. Use COMMAND /C c:\bat\bold instead of the CALL command.

105

Screen Modes

```
@REM  TESTBOLD.BAT
@REM
@REM     ┌─────────────────────────────┐
@REM     │  Test bold and normal type  │
@REM     └─────────────────────────────┘
@SET OLDPROMPT=%PROMPT%
@PROMPT
@ECHO This is normal type
@CALL bold
@ECHO This is BOLD
@CALL normal
@ECHO This is normal type
@SET PROMPT=%OLDPROMPT%
@SET OLDPROMPT=
```

We obtained the following result on the screen with the TESTBOLD.BAT file using the two batch files BOLD.BAT and NORMAL.BAT:

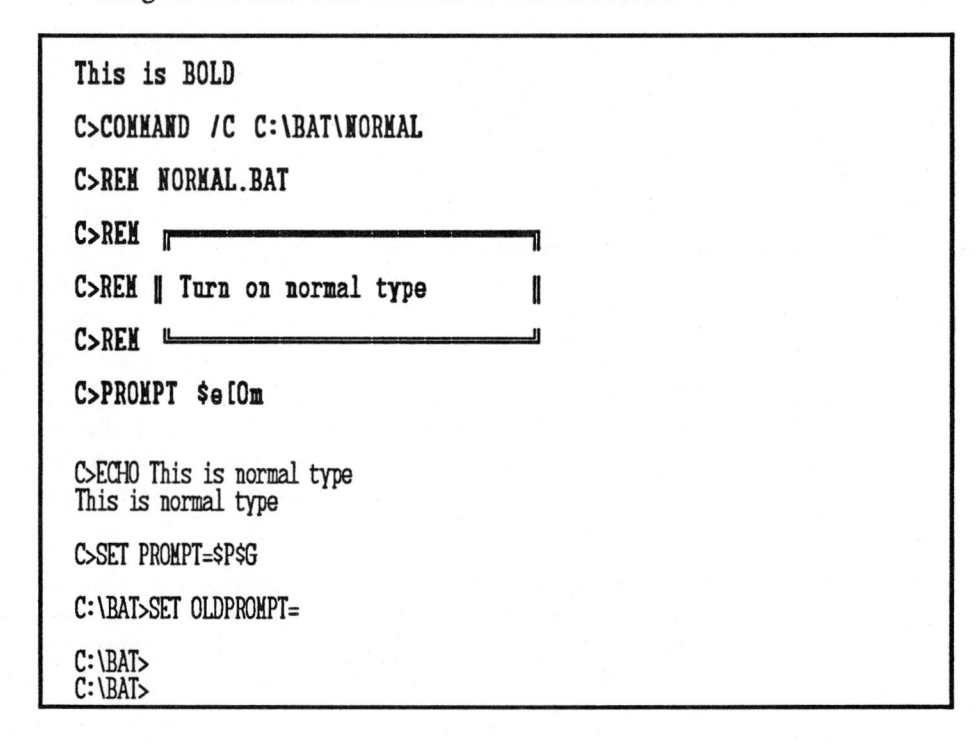

```
This is BOLD

C>COMMAND /C C:\BAT\NORMAL

C>REM NORMAL.BAT

C>REM   ┌─────────────────────────────┐

C>REM   │  Turn on normal type        │

C>REM   └─────────────────────────────┘

C>PROMPT $e[0m


C>ECHO This is normal type
This is normal type

C>SET PROMPT=$P$G

C:\BAT>SET OLDPROMPT=

C:\BAT>
C:\BAT>
```

Fig. 7:   Parts of the Screen Bolded

If you frequently switch back and forth between different character attributes, you shouldn't just add the appropriate escape sequences to the existing prompt with:

@PROMPT %PROMPT%$e[1m

106

You shouldn't do this because the PROMPT string would contain so many letters that you wouldn't be able to read it on the screen. Try this once and look at the new PROMPT string using SET. Call BOLD.BAT and NORMAL.BAT one after the other and then activate SET. You will see the following line:

```
PROMPT=$p$g$e[1m$e[0m
```

To avoid this don't add the escape code to the prompt, but use the old prompt (like the call shown in the previous example), transmit the escape code and then restore the original prompt. The two changed batch files would then look like this:

```
@REM  BOLD.BAT
@REM
@REM  | Turn on bold type |
@REM
@SET  OLDPROMPT=%PROMPT%
@PROMPT $e[1m

@SET  PROMPT=%OLDPROMPT%

@REM  NORMAL.BAT
@REM
@REM  | Turn on normal type |
@REM
@SET  OLDPROMPT=%PROMPT%
@PROMPT $e[0m

@SET  PROMPT=%OLDPROMPT%
```

For these batch files:

- First save the old prompt in a new variable so that you can restore it later.

- Then establish the PROMPT command for ANSI.SYS.

- MS-DOS sends a PROMPT, at the next blank line ("@" does not suppress the display of the prompt) and thereby transmits the control command, contained in the prompt, to ANSI.SYS. This causes ANSI.SYS to switch all further screen output to the desired type.

- After the command has been dispatched, the old prompt can be restored.

Now you can call both batch files as often as you want, without increasing the size of the the prompt. However, you must display at least one command line on the screen because there is no "@" character to suppress the display of the command line.

107

Screen Modes

You can also change the character attributes in certain parts of the prompt or emphasize the prompt while the rest of the line remains in normal type. The following is an illustration of the latter option:

```
PROMPT $e[1m$p$g$e[0m
```

Only the prompt appears in bold type, the rest of the line does not stand out when it is entered.

Explanation

Perhaps you are wondering about "%PROMPT%". While MS-DOS sets the first given parameter for "%1", it sets the contents of the *environment variables* "PROMPT" for "%PROMPT%". These are variables, which are managed by MS-DOS, that have special meanings (i.e., the variable PROMPT, that contains the current system prompt) and additional variables, which are defined by the user. SET allows you to look at the available variables. SET PROMPT="pg" gives the variables the new value "pg" and displays both the drive and path in the prompt.

Inverse Video

The problem

Suppose that you have a monochrome monitor that always displays text in bright letters on a dark background and you want to reverse this to dark letters on a bright background. This can easily be done by using the appropriate PROMPT command.

The solution

Simply use the following command line:

```
PROMPT $e[7m
```

This reverses the colors used to display the letters and the background. Using this prompt will remove the preceding prompt (e.g., the path statement displayed with

"pg"). To retain the existing prompt, use the environment variables in a batch file. The finished batch file with the name INVERT.BAT looks like this:

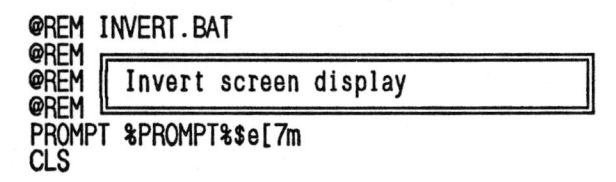

```
@REM  INVERT.BAT
@REM
@REM  | Invert screen display |
@REM
PROMPT %PROMPT%$e[7m
CLS
```

Explanation

The reason for the above example's appearance is the number 7 in the PROMPT command:

```
PROMPT %PROMPT%$e[7m
```

The number 7 instructs DOS to display *inverse video*, in which the background is assigned the character color and the characters are assigned the background color. The CLS command at the end of the INVERT.BAT file changes the entire screen display to inverse video.

Setting character colors

The problem

If you are using a color graphic card in your PC and have a color monitor connected, you can use the PROMPT command and escape sequences to set the color of your characters and background.

The solution

First try the color modifications. For example, to make the color of the characters green, enter the following prompt:

```
PROMPT $p$g$e[32m
```

Screen Modes

Now all of the screen output will appear in green. You can also use the following values:

Value	Type color
30	black
31	red
32	green
33	yellow
34	blue
35	magenta (violet)
36	cyan (green blue)
37	white

It's also possible to change the color of the screen background. For example, to change the background to red, use the prompt:

PROMPT pg$e[41m

The following is a list of the different colors you can use for the background and their corresponding values:

Value	Background color
40	black
41	red
42	green
43	yellow
44	blue
45	magenta (violet)
46	cyan (green blue)
47	white

To change the characters back to white and the background to black, use the following prompt:

Note: If these aren't your original colors, enter the appropriate values.

PROMPT pg$e[37;40m

Explanation

You can set three different specifications, separated by semicolons, and then close the escape sequence with "m". The general call is as follows:

PROMPT pg$e[a;b;cm

For "a" you can set one of the character attributes "0-7", for "b" a character color "30-37" and for "c" a background color "40-47". In order to switch between different attributes frequently, you should use a batch file to do this (as we did in the section "Using character attributes to emphasize text"). This will also enable you to retain the existing prompt (%PROMPT%).

If your PC supports other graphic or text modes you can also change these with ANSI.SYS. Check the documentation that came with your system.

Text or Graphic mode

The problem

You want to switch between text and graphic mode.

The solution

Use the escape code "xh" (depending on the PC's graphic adapter) to choose from the following display modes:

x	Screen display
0	40*25 monochrome
1	40*25 color
2	80*25 monochrome
3	80*25 color
4	320*200 color
5	320*200 monochrome
6	640*200 monochrome

For example, to switch on "40*25 monochrome", use the prompt:

PROMPT $e[0h

Screen Modes

Tip: With certain settings, the screen may automatically clear after any screen display. Enter your normal prompt (e.g., PROMPT pg) and the screen will stop clearing. You should find out which modes are supported by your graphic card.

Explanation

When MS-DOS switches to another screen display, the screen contents are partially deleted. Since the prompt is produced again at the end of each command, the display is switched on again, erasing the screen each time. By setting another prompt, the changed screen display will remain but the screen contents will not be deleted.

Keyboard Tips and Tricks

There are several tips and tricks that can be used with your keyboard. In this chapter we will explain what these tips are and how you can use them.

Using a program to switch off Num Lock

The problem

Some BIOS versions (especially on a PC/AT) automatically switch on the <Num Lock> key after every RESET. This means that only numbers can be entered with the numeric keypad; the cursor control has been switched off. In order to use the numeric keypad for cursor control you must deactivate the <Num Lock> key.

The solution

We have developed a small machine language program, which changes the status of <Num Lock> key each time it is called. However, this doesn't change the LED for the key; AT and 386 keyboards also change the LED (Light Emitting Diode) of the <Num Lock> key.

Enter the following program the same way you would enter a batch file and then store it under the name NUMLOCK.DEB. Make sure there is a blank line between RET and RCX.

Keyboard Tips and Tricks

```
A
MOV AX,0040
MOV DS,AX
MOV AL,[0017]
XOR AL,20
MOV [0017],AL
RET

RCX
000E
NNUMLOCK.COM
W
Q
```

Now use the DEBUG command to transform the commands into a machine language program. Enter the following line:

```
DEBUG <NUMLOCK.DEB
```

Your screen will display text similar to the following message:

```
-A
5D83:0100 MOV AX,0040
5D83:0103 MOV DS,AX
5D83:0105 MOV AL,[0017]
5D83:0108 XOR AL,20
5D83:010A MOV [0017],AL
5D83:010D RET
5D83:010E
-RCX
CX 0000
:000E
-NNOLOCK.COM
-W
Write 000E Bytes
-Q
```

Your display may have another value than "5D83". The DEBUG command has created the finished program, NUMLOCK.COM, which switches between cursor control and numerical input each time it is called. If the cursor control is to be activated after every RESET, you can copy the program into your DOS directory and add the call to the AUTOEXEC.BAT.

Explanation

BIOS saves the contents of the 3 LEDs (Num Lock, Caps Lock, Scroll Lock) in memory location 0040:0017. Each key has a bit that, when set, activates the key. The following chart shows the values for the keys:

Using a program to switch off Num Lock

Key	Bit	Hex	Dec
Num Lock	5	20	32
Caps Lock	6	40	64
Scroll Lock	4	10	16

The machine language program takes the contents of memory location 0040:0017 and switches it for the value of bit 5. Then it writes the changed value into the memory location.

Tip: The layout of the keys is not only determined by which keyboard driver you have loaded. It is also possible to change keys after loading the device driver ANSI.SYS with the CONFIG.SYS file. You can also use keys and combinations of keys that otherwise wouldn't have any effect in MS-DOS.

Backslash assigned to the <F2> key

The problem

The backslash key is used quite often in MS-DOS. Some keyboards have this key in a very awkward location and some international keyboards do not contain this key at all, it must be produced with <Alt> +<92>. Since the <F2> function key usually doesn't have a function, we can use this key to produce the backslash.

The solution

Once again we can use an escape code to solve our problem. Simply enter the following line:

    PROMPT $e[0;60;92p

After pressing the <Enter> key, try the <F2> key immediately. The desired character should be produced. Insert this line, before the line that usually sets the standard prompt, into the AUTOEXEC.BAT. If you don't have such a line in your AUTOEXEC.BAT add the following line after the new one:

115

PROMPT

Tip: With some programs, changing the key layout will prevent the execution of a function that is already defined for that key. If this happens, remove the changed key from AUTOEXEC.BAT and create a batch file named BS.BAT (backslash). If you are using a version of DOS below 3.3, don't use the @ sign in your batch files.

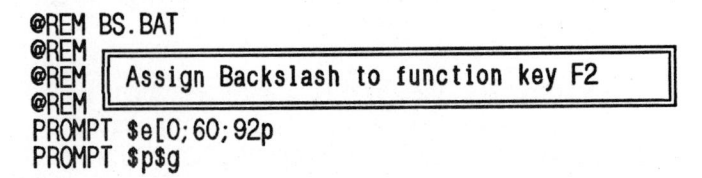

```
@REM  BS.BAT
@REM
@REM  ┌─────────────────────────────────────────┐
@REM  │ Assign Backslash to function key F2     │
      └─────────────────────────────────────────┘
PROMPT $e[0;60;92p
PROMPT $p$g
```

Now you can assign the backslash to function key F2 by entering BS. Next, we will create a second batch named NO_BS.BAT, which cancels the assignment:

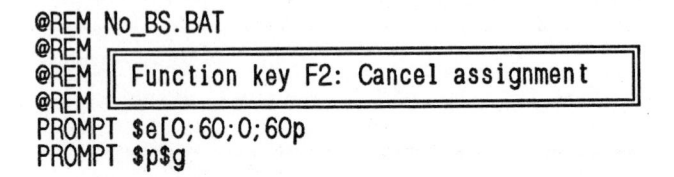

```
@REM  No_BS.BAT
@REM
@REM  ┌─────────────────────────────────────────┐
@REM  │ Function key F2: Cancel assignment      │
      └─────────────────────────────────────────┘
PROMPT $e[0;60;0;60p
PROMPT $p$g
```

Tip: We didn't suppress the screen output using "@" with the PROMPT command because we would have prevented assigning a new function to the key. Next we will show you how to use escape sequences, without the PROMPT command, using ANSI.SYS.

Explanation

You must distinguish between *normal* keys and *extended* keys when you are defining keys. This is important because the operating system has only one number for the normal keys (the ASCII code) while the extended keys contain a 0 and another number. Here is the command for the layout of normal keys:

PROMPT $e[x;yp

For "x" enter the ASCII code of the key you are defining and for "y" enter the new character(s). For one character enter the ASCII value. If there is more than one character, enclose them in quotation marks. The following examples will illustrate this:

PROMPT $e[90;48p	assigns "Z" with the number "0"
PROMPT $e[90;"DIR"p	assigns "Z" with the command "DIR"
PROMPT $e[90;90p	assigns "Z" with "Z"

For "y" (the new character sequence) there are several instructions, separated by semicolons. For example, you can end a command with the <Enter> key by adding the number 13 so that the command will be executed. To do this enter 13 after entering "DIR" in the command line and pressing the <Enter> key. However, the normal keys are not suitable for defining new keyboards since you need them for regular input. Instead, the extended keys should be used.

Escape sequences using COPY

The problem

In order to send the escape sequences via PROMPT to ANSI.SYS, ECHO must be switched to ON. Otherwise the command sequence won't be recognized. By doing this, the screen output will always be displayed. However, it is also possible to send escape sequences without the PROMPT command.

The solution

To send the escape sequences to ANSI.SYS, create a control file (like the one for print commands) with the desired escape code and copy it to the device CON. The problem is getting the ESC character (hex:1B, dec: 27) into the file. There are two ways to do this:

1. You can use the program PRTDAT.BAS from the chapter on printing. This program can create control files. For example, to create the proper escape code for bold type you would have to change line 500 to:

```
500 DATA 27,91,49,109,-1
```

This produces the character sequence "ESC[1m". By starting the BASIC program and entering BOLD.DAT as the filename, you can use the following command line to switch to bold type without changing the prompt:

```
COPY >NUL BOLD.DAT CON
```

ECHO can be switched to OFF the entire time. The following line is shorter and easier to use because you don't have to suppress the COPY command (1 file(s) copied):

```
TYPE BOLD.DAT
```

The following example program creates bold type without changing the prompt and without ECHO:

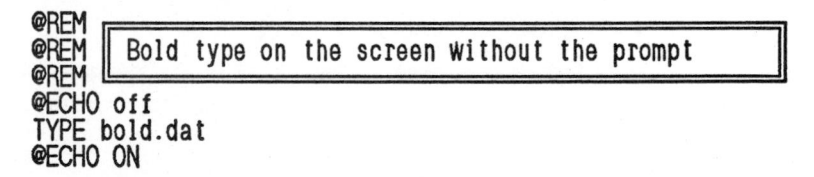

```
@REM
@REM   Bold type on the screen without the prompt
@REM
@ECHO off
TYPE bold.dat
@ECHO ON
```

2. The second solution is useful if you need many different escape sequences. This could make entering the necessary values into the BASIC program PRTDAT.BAS very time consuming. However, all we really need is the ESC character; you can enter the rest of the command characters with any editor or COPY CON. So we will create only the ESC character with the program PRTDAT.BAS. The required line is:

```
500 DATA 27,-1
```

After starting the program enter ESC.DAT as the filename.

Now simply add the rest of the characters (e.g., for bold type "[1m") and you will have a complete control file. You could use COPY CON to copy these three characters into the BOLD file and use:

```
COPY ESC.DAT/a+BOLD BOLD.DAT
```

to link them to a finished escape code.

Explanation

To join the two files, link them in the COPY command with a plus sign. However, if the first file is ended with a file end sign (<Ctrl>+<Z>), it can cause problems (e.g., when using text editors that stop reading the file). Using the option /a instructs MS-DOS to read the file only up to the last character but not to <Ctrl>+<Z>. This combines the data of both files as if they had never been separated.

Commands on the <Alt> key

The problem

Often, while programming, you need special characters, such as the curly braces, graphic lines or the parentheses. However entering these characters with <Alt> and the ASCII code requires a lot of your time. There are also some often used MS-DOS commands that are difficult to enter. These include CD\ and DIR/P. To enter these commands easily, simply assign them to an <Alt> key and a single letter.

The solution

You can solve this problem by using a batch file that creates the necessary escape sequences. If you want to reproduce the original layout of the keys (in case you don't want certain programs to work with the new key layout), we created a second batch file which cancels everything.

```
@REM KEYDEF.BAT
@REM
@REM   Command key layout with ANSI.SYS
@REM
SET OLDPROMPT=%PROMPT%
PROMPT $e[0;60;92p
@REM Backslash to F2
PROMPT $e[0;84;91p
@REM square bracket open on SHIFT + F1
PROMPT $e[0;85;93p
@REM square bracket closed on SHIFT + F2
PROMPT $e[0;86;123p
```

119

Keyboard Tips and Tricks

```
@REM parenthesis open with SHIFT + F3
PROMPT $e[0;87;125p
@REM parenthesis closed with SHIFT + F4
PROMPT $e[0;48;"BACKUP *.* A: /S /M"p
PROMPT $e[0;46;"CD \"p
PROMPT $e[0;32;"DIR /P";13p
PROMPT $e[0;33;"FORMAT A:"p
PROMPT $e[0;50;" | MORE";13p
SET PROMPT=%OLDPROMPT%

@REM OLDKEY.BAT
@REM
@REM   Reproduce old key layout
@REM
SET OLDPROMPT=%PROMPT%
PROMPT $e[0;60;0;60p
PROMPT $e[0;84;0;84p
PROMPT $e[0;85;0;85p
PROMPT $e[0;86;0;86p
PROMPT $e[0;87;0;87p
PROMPT $e[0;48;0;48p
PROMPT $e[0;46;0;46p
PROMPT $e[0;32;0;32p
PROMPT $e[0;33;0;33p
PROMPT $e[0;50;0;50p
SET PROMPT=%OLDPROMPT%
```

You can switch the key layout on and off by storing the first batch under the name KEYDEF.BAT and the second under the name OLDKEY.BAT. The following keys have been assigned by KEYDEF.BAT:

Key	Assignment
F2	Backslash
SHIFT+F1	curly brace open
SHIFT+F2	curly brace closed
SHIFT+F3	parenthesis open
SHIFT+F4	parenthesis closed
ALT+B	BACKUP *.* A: /S /M
	Backup all changed files of the current directory to subdirectories on drive A.
ALT+C	change to main directory
ALT+D	display directory by page (execute immediately)
ALT+F	format disk in drive A
ALT+M	output by page

Explanation

As you can see, the procedure for key layout is self-explanatory. By adding the number 13, you can simulate pressing the <Enter> key, which causes the immediate execution of the command. However this should only be used with "harmless" commands, such as, "PROMPT $e[0;32;"DIR/P;13p". Commands such as the FORMAT command should not be executed automatically.

Now all you need is the remaining special key codes in order to assign all the keys (you can reach the normal characters with the proper ASCII code.) Remember to enter a 0 followed by a semicolon before the special code (i.e., for F1, the sequence is 0;59).

Key	Code	Key	Code
F1	59	F6	64
F2	60	F7	65
F3	61	F8	66
F4	62	F9	67
F5	63	F10	68
F11	53	F12	54
INS	82	HOME	71
DEL	83	END	79
Cursor ←	75	Cursor ↑	72
Cursor →	77	Cursor ↓	80
PgUp	73	PgDn	81
ALT+A	30	ALT+N	49
ALT+B	48	ALT+O	24
ALT+C	46	ALT+P	25
ALT+D	32	ALT+Q	16
ALT+E	18	ALT+R	19
ALT+F	33	ALT+S	31
ALT+G	34	ALT+T	20
ALT+H	35	ALT+U	22
ALT+I	23	ALT+V	47
ALT+J	36	ALT+W	17
ALT+K	37	ALT+X	45
ALT+L	38	ALT+Y	44
ALT+M	50	ALT+Z	21

Keyboard Tips and Tricks

Key	Code	Key	Code
ALT+1	120	ALT+6	125
ALT+2	121	ALT+7	126
ALT+3	122	ALT+8	127
ALT+4	123	ALT+9	128
ALT+5	124	ALT+0	129
ALT+F1	104	ALT+F6	109
ALT+F2	105	ALT+F7	110
ALT+F3	106	ALT+F8	111
ALT+F4	107	ALT+F9	112
ALT+F5	108	ALT+F10	113
ALT+-	130	SHIFT+TAB	15
SHIFT+F1	84	SHIFT+F6	89
SHIFT+F2	85	SHIFT+F7	90
SHIFT+F3	86	SHIFT+F8	91
SHIFT+F4	87	SHIFT+F9	92
SHIFT+F5	88	SHIFT+F10	93
CTRL+F1	94	CTRL+F6	99
CTRL+F2	95	CTRL+F7	100
CTRL+F3	96	CTRL+F8	101
CTRL+F4	97	CTRL+F9	102
CTRL+F5	98	CTRL+F10	103
CTRL+PgUp	132	CTRL+←↓↑	116
CTRL+PgDn	118	CTRL+End	117
CTRL+Print	114	CTRL+Home	119
CTRL+←↓↑	115		

Tip: F11 and F12 are not available in MS-DOS versions lower than 4.0. Don't create too many keyboard layouts because the reserved memory in ANSI.SYS will run out of storage space, which could create some problems.

Updating DOS

Although installing an updated version of MS-DOS seems easy, sometimes it takes a long time for you to use all of the capabilities of the new operating system. In this chapter we will present some tips on how to update your PC to a newer version of MS-DOS.

Installation without a hard drive

Installing an updated version of DOS is easier if you don't have a hard drive. With DISKCOPY, copy the original DOS disk and then store it in a safe place. Now you are ready to adapt the new version of MS-DOS to your needs.

To do this copy the AUTOEXEC.BAT and CONFIG.SYS of your old version of DOS onto the boot disk of the new version. You may receive error messages the first time you boot the new boot disk because the program names have changed.

Installing DOS as a secondary version

The problem

Even if you have problems installing an updated version of DOS, this shouldn't interfere with your work. This is why you should first install the new version as a secondary version on the hard drive.

The solution

If you haven't backed up your hard drive recently, you should do this before updating to a new version of DOS. This is important because your data could be damaged; we will discuss this at the end of this chapter.

Up to MS-DOS version 3.3, this process is simple. Create a new directory and name it DOS33 (for MS-DOS 3.3). Then copy the contents of all the new DOS disks into this directory. Next adapt the AUTOEXEC.BAT and CONFIG.SYS files from the boot disk to your hard drive and new directory. This should look something like the following:

AUTOEXEC.BAT

```
PATH C:\BAT;C:\DOS33
C:\DOS33\KEYB US,437,C:\DOS33\KEYBOARD.SYS
SET COMSPEC=C:\COMMAND.COM
BREAK ON
PROMPT $p$g
```

CONFIG.SYS

```
DEVICE=C:\DOS33\ANSI.SYS
FILES=20
BUFFERS=20
SHELL=C:\DOS33\COMMAND.COM /P /E:990
```

Now you can boot from the new boot disk and work with the programs in the updated MS-DOS version. If there are any problems, you can still boot from the hard disk.

Notes on MS-DOS 4.0 installation procedure

This installation procedure can also be used with MS-DOS 4.0. However, you won't be able to use all of the computer's expanded capabilities immediately (e.g., the new DOS Shell). Make sure to back up all of your data before running the DOS 4.0 installation program.

If you do use this procedure, you can automatically install MS-DOS by booting from the boot disk. However, you must remember the following points when running the SELECT program:

1. Use a new directory, for example C:\DOS40.

2. When you are asked for the directory name you can decide whether to use the new version exclusively or just install it as a secondary version.

    Press the <Tab> key or the cursor to select the desired options and use the <Enter> key to confirm. If you use the pre-set option, all of the MS-DOS commands on your hard drive will be overwritten by the new version and your old version will be lost.

3. If your hard drive is divided into more than one partition, MS-DOS will ask whether this should be changed. Answer no.

    At the end of installation you will have a copy of the boot disk INSTALL and two new files (AUTO.EXEC.400 and CONFIG.400) on the hard disk.

    Copy both of these files onto the boot disk and use the usual extensions (AUTOEXEC.BAT and CONFIG.SYS). You can boot from the boot disk and work with MS-DOS 4.0.

    Tip: In contrast to MS-DOS 4.0, IBM-DOS 4.0 may send the following error message after booting from the boot disk:

    ```
    Invalid media type
    ```

    In this case you can only install DOS after backing up all of the data on the hard disk and then formatting the hard disk from IBM-DOS 4.0. You may not be able to work with any earlier versions of DOS.

Updating DOS

Installing a new version of DOS on the hard drive

The problem

After working with the new version of MS-DOS for a while you may want to permanently install it onto the hard disk C:. In this section we'll discuss the easiest way to do this.

The solution

Assuming that you already have all of the MS-DOS commands in the appropriate directory, all you need to do is make the hard drive bootable for only the new version.

Boot the newest version of DOS from your boot disk. Change the current drive specifier to drive A:. Enter the following to copy the new system files to the hard disk:

```
SYS C:
```

If the installation was a success, MS-DOS displays the following message:

```
System files transferred
```

Now you only need to copy AUTOEXEC.BAT and CONFIG.SYS from the boot disk of the new version onto the hard drive. However, you should save all of the old files so that you can always switch to the old version. Make a boot disk for the old version and copy the old files onto it. If the SYS command responds with an error message, for example:

```
No room for operating system
```

then you won't be able to transfer the new DOS version easily. Also, you will have to format the hard disk with the FORMAT command from the new DOS version. Use the BACKUP command to make a copy of your hard disk onto diskettes. You should save all of your irreplaceable files on separate diskettes in case there are problems with the RESTORE command.

Use the new version of DOS to run the BACKUP, which will enable you to continue working with the saved data. After you have saved all of the data, format the hard disk with the following command:

    FORMAT C: /S

Boot with the new operating system and restore your data on the hard disk with RESTORE. Now the command:

    SYS C:

should correctly transfer the system files to the hard disk and you can copy AUTOEXEC.BAT and CONFIG.SYS onto the hard disk. After a warm boot with <Ctrl> + <Alt> + <Del> the computer should boot from the hard disk without any problems.

Problem solving after installing a new DOS version

The problem

After converting your computer to the new operating system, you encounter some problems and errors.

The solution

Check the AUTOEXEC.BAT and CONFIG.SYS files for the proper settings and PATH statements. If you don't find anything, the following is a list of some other possible causes:

1. Certain programs cannot be called as programs (COM or EXE); you must call them from a batch file. GEM, which is an example of this type of program, is usually started from GEM.BAT.

    During installation a command that determines the location of the *command interpreters* (i.e., SET COMSPEC=C:\COMMAND.COM) is automatically added to the AUTOEXEC.BAT batch file. It's possible that the command interpreter of the old DOS version is in your main directory and the

Updating DOS

AUTOEXEC.BAT.COMSPEC is set to the proper subdirectory of the new DOS version. GEM.BAT will destroy this and MS-DOS will respond with:

`COMMAND.COM invalid`

`COMMAND.COM cannot be loaded, system ended!`

Examine all of the batch files for the key word COMSPEC (see our tip for searching the hard drive for the file contents) and check whether or not the batch file refers to the incorrect command interpreter.

2. Some hard drives and commercial programs require special driver programs (especially with AT and/or hard drives with more than 30 megabytes). These drivers are usually started in the CONFIG.SYS file. If, after changing to a new MS-DOS version with a new CONFIG.SYS file, you can't start the driver, you may see strange error messages like the following:

`Invalid media type.`

Check the CONFIG.SYS of your old MS-DOS version for such drivers (the standard drivers ANSI.SYS, KEYBOARD.SYS, DRIVER.SYS, etc. will be easy to recognize since they are also on the original DOS disks). Then, if necessary, add the proper calls to the new CONFIG.SYS. The hard disk drive manager from Seagate™ is an example of a commercial program that requires the device driver DMDRVR.BIN so that the hard drive can work properly.

3. Many of the utilities and commercial programs that you have installed may also cause problems. It is not guaranteed that these programs will work with a new version of DOS. For example, an early Norton Utilities program, SD.EXE (May 1989), used to optimize the hard disk, produced the following error message after the hard disk was selected under MS-DOS version 4.0:

`Unable to read from drive C`

Many programs that are used to accelerate access to the hard disk (called cache programs) stop working under newer versions of DOS. You can either choose between continuing to work with the old version of DOS (boot from the saved boot disk) or waiting for updated versions of these programs.

4. If you occasionally receive the error message "Incorrect DOS version", then there are still old DOS commands accessible in the PATH statement (this time we won't assume that you have used CD to choose an old DOS directory and called a command). Remove, from the PATH command, all the directories containing old versions of DOS.

The command EXE2BIN, which is used to transform an EXE file into a COM file is also unusual. This command doesn't work with MS-DOS version 3.3 and above. If you try to use this command with a version under DOS 3.3 or DOS 4.0, it will tell you that it is an invalid version of DOS. If you are familiar with DEBUG, you can avoid this problem by changing the 11th byte ($0B) of the program in the following way:

```
DOS 3.2    $14 = 20'
DOS 3.3    $1E = 30
DOS 4.0    $28 = 40
```

Now EXE2BIN should run under the newer versions of DOS.

MS-DOS 4.0 Tips and Tricks

MS-DOS Version 4.0 contains many new options. These options include support for hard disks up to 2 Giga bytes (2*1024 M bytes), easier installation of DOS using the SELECT program, support of the expanded memory (EMS 4.0) and the easy to use DOS Shell. In this chapter we will present some tips that will help you get the most use out of this version. You must have DOS 4.0 installed on your system for these tips and tricks to work. You can use the DOS VER command to check which version of DOS your computer is currently running.

Increasing keyboard speed

The problem

If you have an AT or a 386 machine that has a cursor that either moves too slowly or too quickly over the screen, MS-DOS 4.0 may be able to adjust this speed for you.

The solution

Use the MS-DOS MODE command and select a value for the speed (of key repetition) and a value for the delay (amount of time between repetitions). To do this, enter the following:

```
MODE CON RATE=<Speed> DELAY=<Delay>
```

The values for speed are 1 (slow) through 32 (fast). Delays, which are measured in 1/4 a second, include the values 1 through 4. In order to obtain the highest possible speed from your keyboard, enter the following:

```
MODE CON RATE=32 DELAY=1
```

While trying to adjust your keyboard's speed and delay, you may receive the message:

```
Function is not supported on this computer
```

This means that even MS-DOS cannot help you adjust your keyboard. To permanently change the speed of the keyboard, add the command to your AUTOEXEC.BAT.

Explanation

AT keyboards have their own microprocessors, which can be programmed. This means that ATs receive, from the keyboard, prepared information about the keys that are pressed. The keyboard is also responsible for the speed of key repetition and time of delay until repetition begins.

There are two reasons why you couldn't make these adjustments:

1. The keyboard isn't compatible, which means that it can't understand certain commands from the computer. So, the computer prevents MS-DOS from adapting the desired values.

2. Instead of an AT, you have an XT. Since the XT's keyboard is not programmable, it retains the default values.

The mouse doesn't work in the DOS Shell

The problem

You have a mouse that works perfectly with all of your programs but in the DOS Shell there is no mouse pointer.

The solution

We will assume that you have properly installed the mouse under MS-DOS 4.0 and that you have either placed the mouse driver in the CONFIG.SYS file or that you start the mouse program (MOUSE.COM, GMOUSE.COM etc.) in the AUTOEXEC.BAT file. We'll also assume that you don't have a PS/2 mouse.

Use TYPE to examine the file DOSSHELL.BAT, in your DOS directory. In the file, there should be a long line that begins with "@SHELLC ". If the following text is at the beginning of this line, then DOS Shell assumes that you have a PS/2 mouse:

    /MOS:PCIBMDRV.MOS

Obviously, this won't work. To correct this, simply remove the parameter, /MOS:PCIBMDRV.MOS, from the line.

To do this, save the existing file under DOSSHELL.OLD and then change the line with a word processor. However, do not remove the diagonal backslash "/". You could also use EDLIN to do this but you would have to re-enter the entire line.

When you are finished, save the corrected batch file (as ASCII). Now you shouldn't experience any more problems while using your mouse in the DOS Shell.

Tip: If you have a "compatible" mouse, such as a Logitech mouse or a Genius mouse, but incorrectly entered a Microsoft bus mouse while installing MS-DOS 4.0, try removing the following parameters: /MOS: PCMSDRV.MOS or /MOS:PCMSPDRV.MOS.

Explanation

To call the DOS Shell the DOSSHELL.BAT file should have after "/MOS:", one of three different types of mice:

    PCIBMDRV.MOS   for the IBM PS/2 mouse.
    PCMSDRV.MOS   for the serial Microsoft mouse.
    PCMSPDRV.MOS   for the bus Microsoft mouse.

To call the DOS Shell with one of these parameters, place the mouse driver with the correct name in the DOSSHELL.BAT file. If you have already been working with the mouse outside of the DOS Shell, the old and new drivers may conflict. Simply remove the parameter from the batch file.

Designing a new DOS Shell

The problem

To modify the DOS Shell to fit your needs, you expand the existing commands and groups. However, you can only make the menu points, Command Prompt, File System and Change Colors inactive; you cannot remove them. To do this, remove the parameters /PROMPT, /DOS and /COLOR from the DOSSHELL.BAT batch file. Now create your own DOS Shell by adding your own new menu points.

The solution

Several steps are necessary in order to create your own main group. We will demonstrate these steps by using the example of a main group designed for data processing. For our example, be sure to use the same names we use. If you don't, this procedure might not work. Later, we will explain how you can create a main group that will fit your own needs.

1. In the main group of the DOS Shell create a new group using the menu point, Add in the Group menu. Enter TXTSHELL after "Title:" and also after "Filename:". End the definition by pressing <F2>.

2. Select the group you have just created and add your first program to it with Add from the Program menu:

   ```
   Title:    Command Interpreter
   Command:  COMMAND.COM
   ```

   Use the <F2> key to close this definition. Since you have just added a new program to the group TXTSHELL, MS-DOS will now set up the file TXTSHELL.MEU for the new group.

3. With the <F3> key, leave the DOS Shell. Make a copy of the DOSSHELL.BAT batch file and name this file TXTSHELL.BAT. Change the following contents of the new batch file:

Before	After
@SHELLB DOSSHELL	@SHELLB TXTSHELL
/MEU:SHELL.MEU	/MEU:TXTSHELL.MEU

Save the changed TXTSHELL.BAT file and, instead of calling the DOS Shell with DOSSHELL, use the new batch file, TXTSHELL. Now the only item in the main group is the menu point Command Interpreter, which you created yourself.

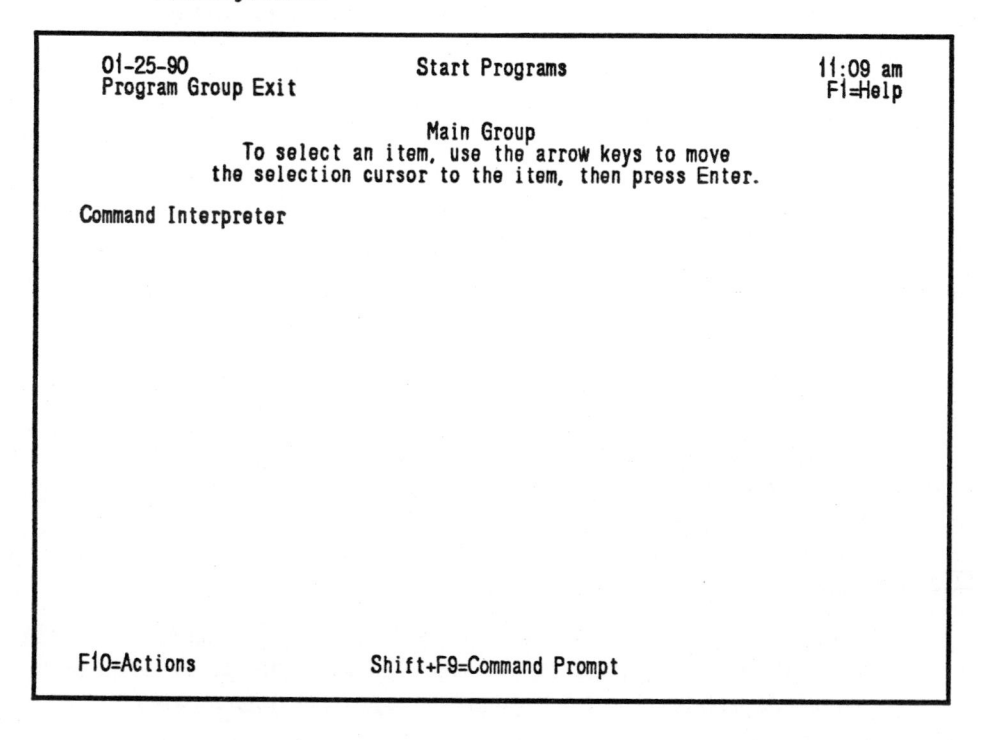

```
01-25-90                  Start Programs                    11:09 am
Program Group Exit                                          F1=Help
                              Main Group
              To select an item, use the arrow keys to move
              the selection cursor to the item, then press Enter.

Command Interpreter




















F10=Actions           Shift+F9=Command Prompt
```

Fig. 8:   Your own Shell

Explanation

You can use any names you want for the batch file and group you create. However, in order for the new group to work, you must remember the following points:

1. You must enter the name (without the BAT ending) of the batch file, from which you call the DOS Shell, on the SHELLB line of the batch file. If the name of the batch file is DOSSHELL.BAT, the line would read:

@SHELLB DOSSHELL

If the name of the batch file is TXTSHELL.BAT (as in our example), then the line would read:

@SHELLB TXTSHELL

2. When entering the filename for the group you have created (in our example TXTSHELL) you must include the ending ".MEU", in the command line to call SHELLB, after the option /MEU:. In our example you would enter:

/MEU: TXTSHELL.MEU

Using functions from the original Shell in your Shell

The problem

You have designed your own Shell but would also like to use a function from the original Shell.

The solution

The easiest way to do this is to create the menu point Command Prompt. We have just added this menu point under the name "Command Interpreter" in the previous example. All you need to do is to output the appropriate reference to EXIT.

To get this reference start your TXTSHELL, move the cursor to the menu point Command Interpreter and choose the menu point Change from the Program menu. Move to the line "Commands" in the window that appears and activate the insert mode by pressing the INSERT key. Now enter:

ECHO Back to SHELL - EXIT and press Enter key

Press the <F4> key at the end of this line and before COMMAND. By doing this you create a double vertical line that separates the commands ECHO and COMMAND. Store the change with <F2> and then try out the menu point.

In contrast to the menu point Command Prompt, the File System and the menu point Change Color cannot be duplicated. Both programs are firmly integrated in the DOS Shell and cannot be started from outside it. You could call another program (PCTOOLS, Norton Utilities) to process files under the appropriate menu point.

It is also easy to duplicate the group DOS Utilities programs (DOSUTIL). Create a group in your own Shell that is identical and then define the same menu points in the new group. Use the submenu point Change to examine the construction of the existing group and menu points so that you have a model for the necessary commands and parameters.

The following tip offers an even easier way to adopt the whole group of "DOS utility programs" to your own DOS Shell.

Linking any group to another Shell

The problem

If you have created several of your own DOS Shells for various purposes, you probably would like to create one group that contains all of the available programs. This can be easily accomplished.

The solution

In the following example we will demonstrate how to do this with the DOS utilities programs (i.e., we will adopt this group into our own Shell). First start the original Shell with DOSSHELL. Then move the cursor to the DOS Utilities programs and choose the menu point Change from the GROUP menu. Remember the term entered after "Filename:"; in our example this is "DOSUTIL".

Use <F3> to leave the DOS Shell and call the Shell you have created (in our example, TXTSHELL). Choose Add in the Group menu. Enter "DOS utility programs" as the title and then the filename you from the normal DOS Shell (in our example, DOSUTIL). Use <F2> to end the process. Now the desired group is in your own Shell and is ready to use. Try it out.

Tip: The information for this group is available only once in the DOSUTIL.MEU file. If you make any changes to this group in your own Shell, the same group in the original Shell will also be affected. To avoid this, copy DOSUTIL.MEU under a different name and enter this name as the filename when you are adding the group.

Adding as many groups as you want

The problem

Unfortunately the DOS Shell allows you to add only groups to the main group and only programs to the group. This not only reduces the number of commands but limits the quantity of definable menu points because you can only have 16 groups or menu points in a group. However, there is a simple trick you can use to avoid this limitation.

The solution

Before showing you the solution, we will perform a short experiment. We will assume that you have created the new DOS Shell TXTSHELL and that you have added the DOS utility programs from the original group to this Shell.

Use DOSSHELL to call the old DOS Shell from the command interpreter. The group you created (TXTSHELL) should be listed in the main group. Select this group. You will be surprised to see that not only do you have the menu point Command interpreter, but also a new group called "DOS utility programs", which can be identified by the three periods that follow its name.

Adding as many groups as you want

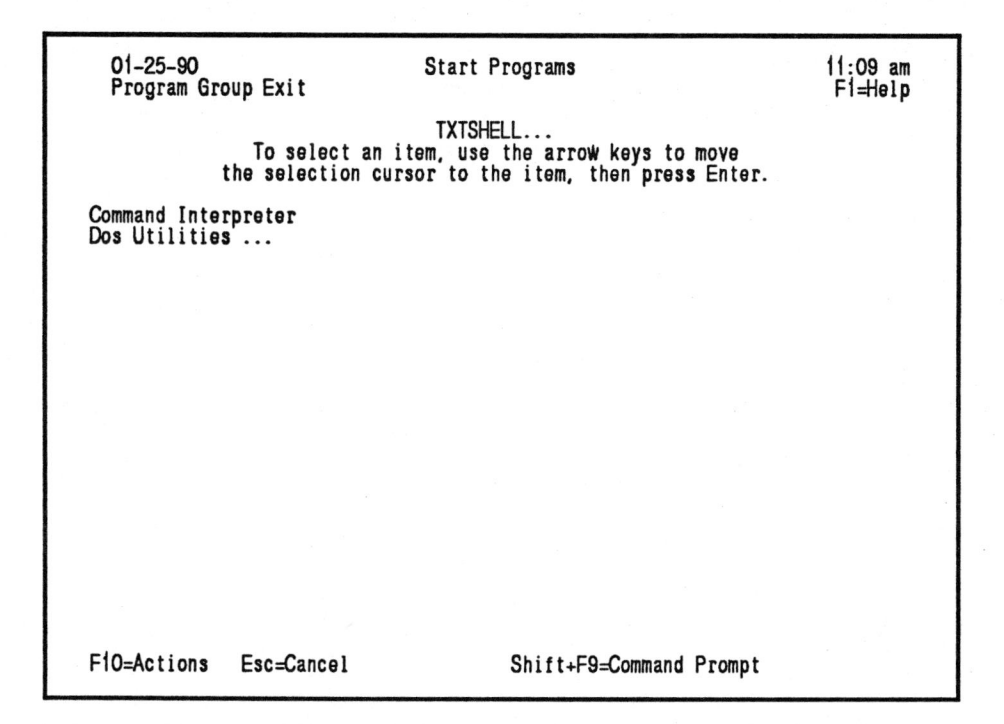

```
  01-25-90                    Start Programs                    11:09 am
  Program Group Exit                                             F1=Help
                                 TXTSHELL...
                     To select an item, use the arrow keys to move
                     the selection cursor to the item, then press Enter.

 Command Interpreter
 Dos Utilities ...













  F10=Actions   Esc=Cancel            Shift+F9=Command Prompt
```

Fig. 9:   Creating a menu group within a group

Result: You have defined a group within the group.

Here is the procedure for building groups within groups:

1. Define a new group in the DOS Shell and remember the filename.

2. Put at least one program in this group so that MS-DOS 4.0 has to store the group contents as a file with the ending ".MEU".

3. Leave the DOS Shell and make a copy of DOSSHELL.BAT. On the copy, change the filename that comes after SHELLB and the parameter line for the DOS Shell /MEU:SHELL.MEU to your own filenames.

4. Call your new Shell with this new batch file. When you define a new group in the main group of this Shell it will also be a group of the subgroup in the original Shell.

5. To add more groups start at step 1. Use your new Shell instead of the original and use your newly created batch file instead of DOSSHELL.BAT.

Tip: Each time you add new groups you must use new filenames for the group and the batch. You should also keep an interim batch, which can be used to turn a group into a main group, because it's the only way to change subgroups. It's possible to choose subgroups of groups from the original Shell but the menu points Add and Change (under: Group) remain inactive.

Defining commands of any length in the DOS Shell

The problem

When you create a new menu point, you can enter one or more MS-DOS commands after Commands. Use two vertical lines (by pressing <F4>) to separate each command. The DOS Shell provides 500 characters for these command lines, but in many cases this is not enough (e.g., when several ECHO lines are desired).

The solution

You can use the command line to call COM or EXE programs or batch files. Since batch files can be as long as you want, you are not restricted to command line length restrictions in the DOS Shell.

However, in a DOS Shell command line, you can't call batch files with the name of the batch. If you do, your batch file will end when you reach the end of the batch file that was called. Instead, you must use the CALL command. For example, to call the batch file FINDALL.BAT, with the parameter .TXT, use the following command:

```
CALL FINDALL  .TXT
```

The command lines in the DOS Shell work like batch files and are governed by the same rules. For DOS versions up to and including 3.2 there is a different line instead of the CALL command:

```
COMMAND.COM /C FINDALL   .TXT
```

You can also use other elements of batch files in the command lines of the DOS Shell. For example, prompts with IF can be used, as in the following batch file:

```
IF EXIST DOSSHELL.BAT TYPE DOSSHELL.BAT
ECHO End of program
PAUSE
```

This corresponds to the following command line in the DOS Shell:

```
IF EXIST DOSSHELL.BAT TYPE DOSSHELL.BAT ‖ ECHO End of program ‖ PAUSE
```

You have to press the <F4> key for each new command line of every line.

User protection in MS-DOS 4.0

The problem

The DOS Shell makes working with MS-DOS much easier, especially for beginners. One advantage is that you can prevent users from accessing certain features, which in turn, can prevent data from being destroyed or altered. Along with the tips we have already given in the chapter on user protection, here are are some special tips and tricks for MS-DOS 4.0.

The solution

First we will briefly discuss several tricks that MS-DOS 4.0 contains which can help with your data security. Then we will focus on the improvements and extensions of these tricks.

Passwords

Passwords can be installed for programs and groups. When you create or change programs and groups, use a password as your last entry. Then you can activate or change the program or group only by entering the passwords into an extra window that will appear.

MS-DOS 4.0 Tips and Tricks

So you can protect all the DOS utility programs with a password. To remove a password, simply erase the entered term from the appropriate line of the window. Obviously you can only do this after entering the password.

Unfortunately, passwords provide only limited protection. All the data of a group are stored in the file named "Filename", which has the ending ".MEU". The main group's file is usually called SHEL.MEU. The files with the ending ".MEU", contain all the stored data that you entered when creating the menu point in the window. They appear in the following sequence:

- Help Text
- Title
- Password
- Command (in Programs)
  Filename (in Groups)

For example, if you use the password MASTER for the group DOS utility programs and store it with <F2>, you can select the file SHELL.MEU in the file system and look at the contents with View File. While paging through the file, you will find the password after "DOS utilities...".

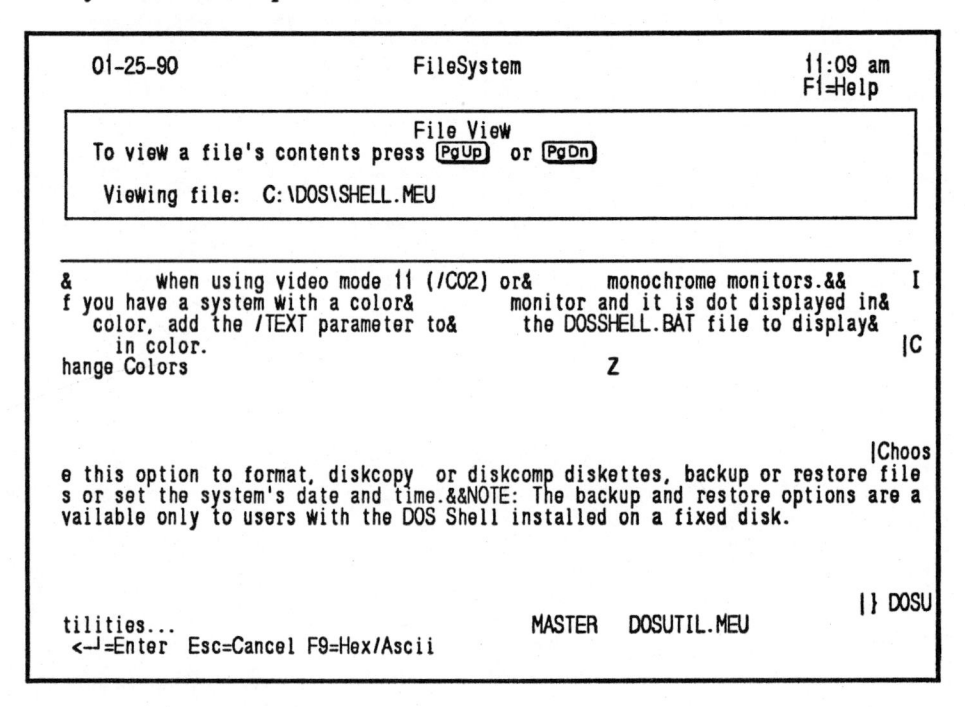

```
 01-25-90              FileSystem                  11:09 am
                                                   F1=Help
 ┌──────────────────── File View ────────────────────────┐
 │ To view a file's contents press [PgUp] or [PgDn]      │
 │                                                        │
 │ Viewing file:  C:\DOS\SHELL.MEU                        │
 └────────────────────────────────────────────────────────┘


  &       when using video mode 11 (/C02) or&    monochrome monitors.&&       I
 f you have a system with a color&         monitor and it is dot displayed in&
    color, add the /TEXT parameter to&     the DOSSHELL.BAT file to display&
       in color.                                                             |C
 hange Colors                                   Z



                                                                        |Choos
 e this option to format, diskcopy  or diskcomp diskettes, backup or restore file
 s or set the system's date and time.&&NOTE: The backup and restore options are a
 vailable only to users with the DOS Shell installed on a fixed disk.


                                                                        |} DOSU
  tilities...                         MASTER   DOSUTIL.MEU
    <─┘=Enter  Esc=Cancel F9=Hex/Ascii
```

Fig. 10: *It's so easy to find a password*

User protection in MS-DOS 4.0

If the file system is also protected by a password you can still use the TYPE command from the command interpreter. The display of the file SHELL.MEU will not be very clear but you can easily see the password.

Protecting Passwords

If it is so easy to find the correct password, why not arrange for the wrong password to be displayed? You can do this by inserting a special character into the password.

To do this, begin the password with a blank, <Alt> + <255> (use the numerical key pad to enter the numbers). This character looks exactly like a space, but MS-DOS can easily distinguish it from the space created with the ASCII value 32. To make such an entry, do the following:

1. Enter <Alt> + <255>; it will appear as a space on the screen.

2. Enter the remaining characters (up to 7) of the password.

If someone tries to find the password with TYPE or from the file system, it will be difficult to enter the password properly.

Deactivating Elements of the DOS Shell

Another advantage of the DOS Shell is that you can prevent access to important elements by deactivating them. You may have wondered about the long command line in the DOSSHELL.BAT batch file. Many of the parameters entered in this line allow access to the most important control elements of the Shell. The following is list of parameters, and their meanings, that can be used for user protection:

/EXIT   Without this parameter it is impossible to leave the DOS Shell by pressing the <F3> key or selecting Exit Shell in the Exit menu.

/PROMPT Without this parameter it is impossible to leave the Shell by selecting Command Prompt or <Shift> + <F9>.

/MENU   Without this parameter you can only work with the File System. You automatically start the File System by calling the Shell. When you leave you return to the command interpreter.

/MAINT   Without this parameter all of the menu points except Start, under Program and Exit Shell, under Exit are deactivated. You cannot add, change or erase programs or groups.

/DOS   Without this parameter access to the File System is deactivated.

/COLOR   Without this parameter you cannot change the colors of the DOS Shell.

What's the Best Way to Set Up Protective Mechanisms?

Suppose a friend is going to use your computer but you only want him/her to be able to work with the word processor and to copy files from the hard disk onto floppy disks. Use the following procedure:

1. As described in this chapter, create a new DOS Shell with the start file DOSSHELL.BAT.

2. Give the new Shell three menu points:

   ```
   1. Starting the COMMAND.COM.
   2. Starting the word processor.
   3. Copying files from the hard disk onto floppy disks.
   ```

3. Protect the first menu point (Starting the COMMAND.COM) with a password.

4. Remove the following menu points from the call for your new Shell: /PROMPT /EXIT /MAINT /DOS.

5. Modify your AUTOEXEC.BAT so that at the end of your last command, the batch file, which starts your custom Shell, is called.

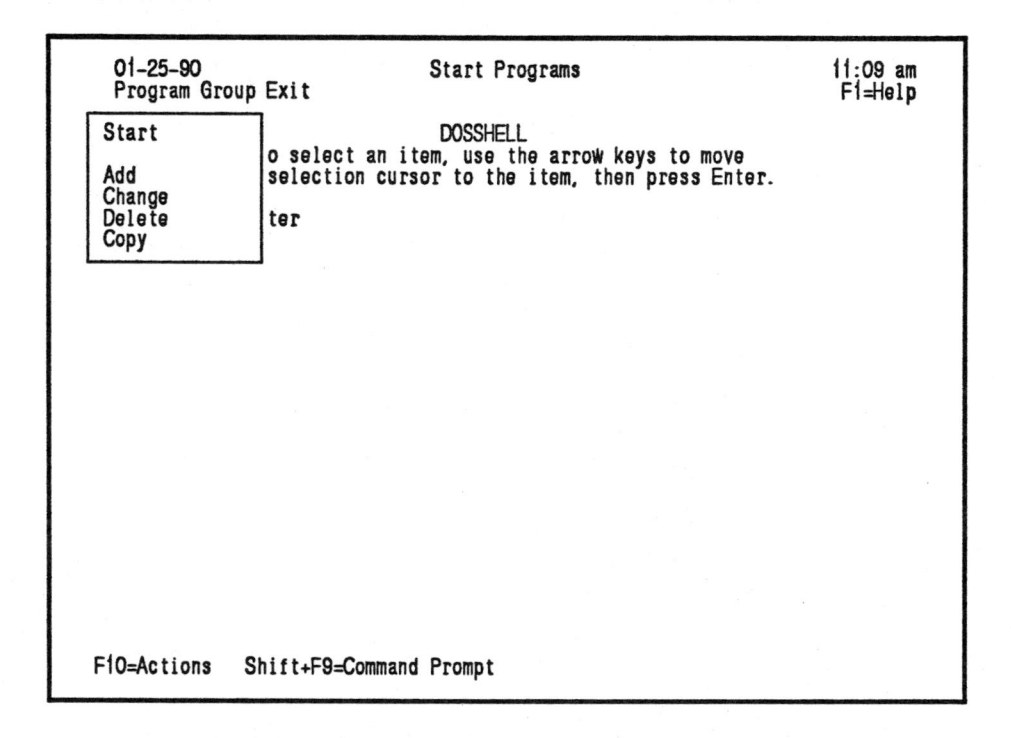

```
    01-25-90                   Start Programs                11:09 am
    Program Group Exit                                       F1=Help
   ┌─────────────┐
   │ Start       │              DOSSHELL
   │             │ o select an item, use the arrow keys to move
   │ Add         │ selection cursor to the item, then press Enter.
   │ Change      │
   │ Delete      │ ter
   │ Copy        │
   └─────────────┘










   F10=Actions    Shift+F9=Command Prompt
```

Fig. 11: A protected DOS Shell; Add , Change, Delete, and Copy deactivated

Now when you work on your computer, you can use the password to start the command interpreter from the DOS Shell, which gives you free access to the computer, or you can boot from your own boot disk. The computer will be protected from unauthorized use since no other options can be selected.

Backing up data

Perhaps you wouldn't expect a chapter on how to backup data to appear in a MS-DOS tips and tricks book. However, if weeks or months worth of your data was ever destroyed, and you have backup copies of your work, you would probably be very grateful. In this chapter we will show you the most reliable methods for backing up your data. Before we begin, we will discuss two myths:

Data cannot be destroyed only by DEL or FORMAT

Many people think that the only way to destroy data is to accidentally enter DEL *.* or FORMAT C:. However, we don't believe these commands are very harmful because most users are aware of the hazards they represent. The worst thing DEL *.* could do is destroy the files in the current directory. But there are special tools that can be used to undo this command. Most DOS versions also allow you to stop FORMAT C: without losing any data.

The following are examples from our own experiences. As you will see, they will demonstrate that there are much worse dangers for your data.

1. Suddenly you have trouble with your hard disk. It is obvious that there is a defect in the hard disk controller and the hard disk can only write data, not read it. Since you desperately need the data, you call your computer dealer who promises to help. In the confusion, you forget to secure (park) the hard disk before taking it to the dealer. When you arrive, the PC refuses to work with the hard disk. You find that the Read/Write element has cracked open on the disk and has destroyed irreplaceable system data. All of your data are now permanently lost.

2. Suddenly the word processor crashes while your manuscript is being stored. At first, this doesn't seem to be a problem because BAK files (backup copies of the existing file) are automatically created. Then MS-DOS starts to act strangely when the PC is rebooted and responds with several error messages. CHKDSK shows over 2000 lost clusters and most of the files on the hard

disk are empty or useless. In addition to everything else, there are no backup copies.

3. After inadvertently erasing a file, you vaguely remember that you can cancel this command. You suddenly remember the RECOVER command. When you look at your screen after entering RECOVER C:, the following message appears on the screen:

```
To recover File(s) from drive C: press a key
```

which indicates that the RECOVER command will take care of the problem. Unfortunately since you didn't backup all of your files, they are lost. The following message alarms you:

```
329 File(s) recovered
```

You had only erased one file but when you look in the directory you realize what happened. All of the files on the hard disk were numbered in order from FILE0001.REC to FILE0329.REC in the main directory of the hard disk. There are no more subdirectories.

Perhaps these examples have convinced you that the data on your hard disk are about as safe as a wallet in a room full of pickpockets.

Backing up data doesn't have to be time consuming and complicated

Often the commands DISKCOPY A: B: and BACKUP C: A: /S come to mind when you think of backing up your data. However, in many cases, there are better ways to backup your data than placing 31 backup diskettes into drive A: every week.

Here are some ways of protecting your data that are quick, safe and easy.

Backing up data quickly and easily

The problem

The BACKUP command requires many diskettes to backup all the files on a hard disk. Besides the BACKUP command, there are other ways to backup your data.

Backing up the last file you worked with

The easiest way to backup one or a few files is to copy them directly onto a disk with COPY. After finishing and storing a file or text, copy the file(s) onto a special backup disk. Depending on the size of the files and the different types of work you do on your PC, one backup disk is adequate for the current data or several backup disks for different types of work.

This simple method doesn't take much time and protects you from losing all of the data on the hard disk. Also, you have direct access to the backed up files and don't need to put all of the backup copies in a large series of backup diskettes.

Backing up several files you have changed

If you work with several files each day, copying each file with COPY could take a long time. You could write a batch file to copy single files, but this isn't practical unless you always use the same filenames.

If all of the data will fit onto one disk, secure them by using XCOPY. Every time you change the file, MS-DOS will set an Archive Flag. This flag indicates whether or not the file has been changed since the last time you saved it.

For example, to secure all of the text files, from the directory C:\TEXTS, that have been changed since the last time you backed them up, use the following command:

```
XCOPY C:\TEXTS\*.TXT A: /m
```

The /m parameter indicates that only the files that haven't been secured (Archive Flag) should be copied and that the flags should be reset (they indicate that files have been secured).

If there are other subdirectories, located in the directory, that contain files you want to secure, simply enter /s as an additional parameter.

Besides being quick, this procedure also provides direct access to the backup copies in case the original files are destroyed.

Using BACKUP properly

The problem

Many MS-DOS users complain that BACKUP is inadequate and awkward to use. However, when used with a few tricks, this command can produce excellent results.

Backup only what you need

Since BACKUP is not very fast, it might take you several hours to backup a full 20Mb hard disk. This is why you should decide which files really need to be backed up and then backup only these files. The following procedure is the best way to do this:

1. First backup the entire hard disk with:

    BACKUP C:*.* A: /S

    Now all of the files in all of the subdirectories are backed up. With MS-DOS 3.3 and above, you should also add the /f parameter because BACKUP will then pre-format the backup diskettes. All MS-DOS versions below 3.3 are unable to preformat diskettes.

    If you should lose the entire contents of the hard disk, you can restore them with RESTORE. Points 2 and 3 describe the procedure for backing up the current versions of your changed files.

2. To backup additional work, specify the directories whose data you are changing. This avoids having to backup the DOS directory or your programs

Using BACKUP properly

with every BACKUP because you have already secured them as originals and in a general full disk backup.

An even easier way to secure your data is by installing one directory (C:\DATA) with the corresponding subdirectories for all of the files that you frequently use. Then you can backup your data quickly by entering the following line:

    BACKUP C:\DATA*.* A: /S

3. Instead of backing up the entire directory C:\DATA, you can save time by backing up only the files that you have changed since the last time you backed up data. Call BACKUP with the following command line:

    BACKUP C:\DATA*.* A: /S /M /A

Insert the last disk from the backup you performed in step 2 and have the other disks ready. BACKUP will now backup all of the files that haven't yet been backed up. If the disk fills up you have to insert another empty disk.

This method of securing current changes is quick and easy. However, you shouldn't use it too often because you might accumulate too many disks. Backup the DATA directory again with step 2.

The correct way to RESTORE

The problem

You can restore lost data with RESTORE. However, there are some things you should remember when using this command.

Restoring a file

If a file is lost (e.g. C:\DATA\TEXTS\BOOK) from the hard disk you can easily restore it, from the backup of C:\DATA, with RESTORE:

    RESTORE A: C:\DATA\TEXTS\BOOK.TXT

151

Backing up data

RESTORE will then repeatedly ask you to insert the backup copies until it finds the file it is looking for and restores it onto the hard disk.

Restoring several files

If a considerable number of files have been destroyed or erased, for example all of the files in the directory C:\DATA\TEXTS, you can use RESTORE with wildcards. However, you should be careful when doing this. For example, if you enter:

```
RESTORE A: C:\DATA\*.*
```

all of the files will be replaced with backup copies. This means that any changes made to the files since the last time they were backed up will be lost.

There are two different procedures depending on the type of data loss:

1. If the files on the hard disk have been completely erased, use the /n parameter. This restores, from the backup disks, only the files that are no longer in the original directory. For example:

   ```
   RESTORE A: C:\DATA\*.* /N
   ```

2. If you cannot find a suitable wildcard for the files, then remember the files that you have to restore and call RESTORE in the following manner:

   ```
   RESTORE A: C:\DATA\*.* /p
   ```

   This causes RESTORE to ask, for all the files that have been changed since the last backup, whether or not the file in question should be replaced.

Caution: Don't lose your data with RESTORE

Tip: If you have already lost files, you obviously don't want to cause more damage while restoring the files. To avoid this, make an additional BACKUP of the directory that has lost the data so that you can cancel any damages caused by incorrect restoration.

When RESTORE doesn't work

What if you used RESTORE to restore data, inserted all of the disks, but received the following message at the end of the program:

```
No files found to restore
```

You probably made a mistake while entering the path or filename or you used the wrong wildcard(s).

There is also another reason for this error message. You may have tried to restore data into another directory, which isn't possible. If you backed up data from C:\DATA, you can't restore them in a C:\BAK directory.

Note: Write the pathname of the secured directory on the disk or use the following tip about the control file.

Checking backup data with a control file

The problem

Suppose that you are working with many different backups to save time but you can't remember which files have been backed up on which disks. There is an easy solution.

The solution

When you are creating backups, keep the information about all of the copied files in a file called BACKUP.LOG. Use /L as your parameter. To backup all of the files in C:\DOS with the subdirectories and keep these files in BACKUP.LOG, use the command line:

    BACKUP C:\DOS*.* A: /S /L

It would also be helpful if you stored all of the LOG files under a meaningful name in a special directory, for example C:\LOG. You will immediately notice the advantages of doing this. First, let's look at a LOG file created by BACKUP:

Backing up data

```
6/27/1989  21.16.18
001   \DOS\ANSI.SYS
001   \DOS\CONFIG.SYS
001   \DOS\COUNTRY.SYS
001   \DOS\DISPLAY.SYS
001   \DOS\DRIVER.SYS
001   \DOS\EMM.SYS
001   \DOS\EMM386.SYS
001   \DOS\EMMOLD.SYS
001   \DOS\HIMEM.SYS
001   \DOS\KEYBOARD.SYS
001   \DOS\NEATEMM.SYS
001   \DOS\PRINTER.SYS
001   \DOS\QEMM.SYS
001   \DOS\RAMDRIVE.SYS
001   \DOS\RDISK.SYS
001   \DOS\SEEMS.SYS
001   \DOS\SEMS4.SYS
001   \DOS\SMARTDRV.SYS
001   \DOS\XMA2EMS.SYS
002   \DOS\XMA2EMS.SYS
```

At the beginning of the file, BACKUP records the date and time the data was backed up. Then it lists all of the files and their paths. The three digit number before the filename represents the number of backup diskette.

If you create another backup, BACKUP will append these data to an existing BACKUP.LOG file. To create a LOG file for every backup, either rename BACKUP.LOG or enter the filename of the LOG file after the /l parameter. However there is a catch to the latter method. The first character after /l will be ignored by BACKUP. Enter:

```
BACKUP C:\DATA\*.* A: /S /LTEXT.LOG
```

The LOG file will read TEXT.LOG. There are two advantages to preserving all of the LOG files in the C:\LOG directory:

1. By reading the date of the LOG file you can always determine the last time you backed up certain files.

2. You can use the FINDTEXT.BAT batch file to search for a file in your LOG files and immediately discover the location of the file.

Recovering data

The problem

Backing up data doesn't always protect them from being lost. Sometimes you must try to recover data, for example when data are lost and an error appears on the backup disks.

The solution

MS-DOS doesn't have many ways of recovering data. The following are two methods that have been successful in many instances.

Reading errors on the disk

You want to use data from a backup disk but receive one of the following error messages:

```
General Failure reading drive A
Abort, Retry, Ignore, Fail

Irrecoverable Error reading drive A:, page 0, track 16
```

If you don't have any copies of the files but you need the data, simply make a copy of the defective disk and try the same process with the copy. With a little luck you will be able to read most of the data from the defective disk.

Tip: If you have ever recovered data in this way you should check them carefully. It's possible that the files are no longer in order. For example, different characters could appear.

If copying the disk doesn't help, you can try the RECOVER command, which we will describe in the next section.

Reading errors on the hard disk

If you can't use the data on your hard disk and don't have any copies on backup, you can try using RECOVER. This command will attempt to recover what it can from one or more files.

155

Caution: RECOVER is dangerous and can cause much damage if it isn't used properly. Before you try RECOVER you should backup the volume by copying the disk or by making a backup of the hard drive.

If you know the name of the file that can't be read you can call RECOVER, using the filename as a parameter. RECOVER changes the defective file into one or more files, such as FILE0000.CHK, FILE0001.CHK, etc. This divides the file into several readable sections. The sections you can't read are lost.

You can also use RECOVER on an entire drive if you have several unreadable files on a disk or on the hard drive. RECOVER will then continue to restore as much data as possible and place them in consecutively numbered files such as FILE????.CHK.

Caution: Since RECOVER cannot distinguish between files that are useful and files that are defective, all of the files are included in this procedure. Remember that RECOVER doesn't use meaningful filenames and that all of the files will be located in the main directory; the entire structure of your directory will be destroyed. So it is important that you backup all of the intact files beforehand.

Use RECOVER on the hard drive when you can do without most of the data (because they have already been backed up) and especially when you must have data that's not backed up. To find your way back to these files, use the methods described in the chapter on "Searching files". These methods will help you search all the files of a directory or even the files of a volume for certain contents.

The following are a few additional tips to help you with this problem: After recovering all of the data from the volume you should reformat the volume so that the defective sectors are no longer used. You cannot recover any structured data with RECOVER. For example, if you try to recover a formatted WORD text that RECOVER has separated into several partial files, not only will you barely be able to process these partial files with WORD, but WORD might abort while you are trying to read them. The same is true for the structured data of a database, similar files and operable programs.

Finally, remember that in addition to MS-DOS, there are other ways of recovering data. For example, you might want to purchase a tool for recovering data, such as PC TOOLS or Norton Utilities, etc.

Analysis of a backup - What is on a backup diskette?

The problem

Suppose that a while ago you backed up part of your hard disk, but without making a LOG file or taking good notes. How do you find out which files are on a backup disk?

The solution

Beginning with MS-DOS 3.3, there are two files in the main directory of every backup disk:

```
Volume in drive A is BACKUP   001
Directory of   A:\

BACKUP    001     360796  24.05.89  14.19
CONTROL   001        379  24.05.89  14.19
        2 file(s)         0 Bytes free
```

BACKUP.001 contains the actual secured data while the second file, CONTROL.001 contains important information about the directories and files of the secured data on the disk. If you try to look at the contents of the CONTROL.001 file by using

    TYPE A:CONTROL.001

many strange characters will appear on the screen. If you're lucky, you might be able to discover some filenames in between these characters. This happens because BACKUP stores the data in a special form that's difficult to read. This is why we wrote the LISTBACK.BAS program, which will display the information contained in the CONTROL file in an easy to understand format.

In contrast to the RESTORE command in MS-DOS, this method enables you to go directly to the contents of any disk, for example disk 14. All you have to do is, at the start, give the disk number to the program. Test this now by using DIR to look at the extensions of both files.

Backing up data

Unfortunately there is one small drawback to this method. The programs LISTBACK.BAS and GETBACK.BAS (introduced in the next tip) cannot be written in GWBASIC. The reason for this is that in GWBASIC it is impossible to read files at will. For example, if the character <Ctrl> + <Z> (ASCII code 26) appears in the file, the file is finished according to GWBASIC - even if there are more data to be read. Therefore, we had no other choice but to develop these programs in Microsoft's QuickBASIC.

In QuickBASIC, on the other hand, you can read files in a way that is not subject to these restrictions. If you don't have QuickBASIC, ask some of your friends and associates. If someone can compile both programs for you, you could use them without QuickBASIC. The companion disk for this book contains both the BASIC source code and the QuickBASIC compiled programs.

```
REM LISTBACK.BAS
CLS
PRINT "***************************************************************"
PRINT "*    Program to show files from a Backup-Set                 *"
PRINT "*    (V3.3)                                                  *"
PRINT "*                         by Manfred Tornsdorf               *"
PRINT "***************************************************************"
PRINT "Press any key..."
Start:
INPUT "Please enter Disk Number"; DiskNr
IF DiskNr < 1 OR DiskNr > 999 THEN PRINT " Inadmissible Num. (1-999)": GOTO Start
DiskNr$ = STR$(DiskNr)
DiskNr$ = MID$(DiskNr$, 2, LEN(DiskNr$) - 1)
WHILE LEN(DiskNr$) < 3
DiskNr$ = "0" + DiskNr$
WEND
Controlfile$ = "a:\CONTROL." + DiskNr$

REM Check whether right disk has been inserted
ON ERROR GOTO Derror
OPEN Controlfile$ FOR INPUT AS #1
CLOSE #1
ON ERROR GOTO 0
OPEN Controlfile$ FOR BINARY AS #1
REM ******************* Read header of Control file **************
DoDisk:
Num = 1: REM Read length bytes of the header
GOSUB Readit
PRINT "Length of header = "; HEX$(Na)
HeaderLen = Na
Num = 8: REM Name
GOSUB Readit
PRINT "Name = "; N$
Num = 1: REM Disk_number
GOSUB Readit
PRINT "Disk number of the backups = "; Na
Num = HeaderLen - 10: REM Read remaining headers
GOSUB Readit
```

Analysis of a backup - What is on a backup diskette?

```
REM ****************** read data sentence **********************
GetBlock:
WHILE INKEY$ = "": WEND
PRINT
Num = 1: REM length(70 = dir, 34 = file)
GOSUB Readit
Blocklen = Na: REM   REM Note length
IF Blocklen = 0 THEN GOTO Ende
IF Na = 70 THEN
PRINT "Directory: "; : REM ******************* Directory
Num = 63: REM read directory name
GOSUB Readit
Dirname$ = N$
PRINT Dirname$: REM output name
Num = 1: REM LowByte read num files
GOSUB Readit
Numfile = Na
Num = 1: REM Highbyte
GOSUB Readit
Numfile = Numfile + 256 * Na
PRINT "Number of files in directory on disk = "; Numfile
Num = 4: REM Read remaining bytes  (Address next directory or FF FF)
GOSUB Readit
GOTO GetBlock
ELSE
IF Na = 34 THEN
PRINT "File:"; : REM ****************** File
Num = 12: REM read file name
GOSUB Readit
PRINT N$
Num = 1: REM Split-Byte (3=complete, 2=remainder follows) read
GOSUB Readit
IF Na = 2 THEN PRINT "File incomplete, continue on next disk"
FileLen = 0
Factor = 1
FOR I = 1 TO 4
Num = 1
GOSUB Readit
FileLen = FileLen + Na * Factor
Factor = Factor * 256
NEXT I
PRINT "File length = "; FileLen
Num = 2: REM two Bytes (01,00)
GOSUB Readit
Filestart = 0
Factor = 1
FOR I = 1 TO 4
Num = 1
GOSUB Readit
Filestart = Filestart + Na * Factor
Factor = Factor * 256
NEXT I
PRINT "File start address = "; Filestart
filelendisk = 0
Factor = 1
FOR I = 1 TO 4
Num = 1
GOSUB Readit
```

Backing up data

```
        filelendisk = filelendisk + Na * Factor
        Factor = Factor * 256
        NEXT I
        PRINT "File length of this disk = "; filelendisk

        Num = 6: REM attribute, date etc.
        GOSUB Readit
        Numfile = Numfile - 1
        IF Numfile = 0 THEN
        PRINT "--------------------------------"
        END IF
        GOTO GetBlock
        ELSE
        PRINT "Error, wrong block length:"; Na
        END IF: REM IF 34
        END IF: REM IF 70 OR 34

        Ende:
        PRINT "Program end"
        CLOSE #1
        END

        Readit:
        N$ = INPUT$(Num, #1)
        Na = ASC(N$ + CHR$(0))
        RETURN

        Derror:
        BEEP
        PRINT "Please insert the correct disk and press any key"
        PRINT "(E=End)..."
        waithere:
        Check$ = INKEY$
        IF Check$ = "" THEN GOTO waithere
        IF Check$ = "e" OR Check$ = "E" THEN CLOSE : END
        RESUME
```

Enter the disk number after the start of the program. After inserting the first disk of a backup, you will see the following after entering "1":

```
    Length of the header = 8B
    Name = BACKUP
    Disk number of the backup = 1
```

After pressing a key the first secured directory of this disk and the number of files available will be displayed. For example:

```
    Directory: DOS
    Number of files in directory on this disk = 5
```

When you press a key, the first file of the disk will display something similar to:

```
File: ANSI.SYS
File length = 1647
File start address = 0
File length of this disk = 1647
```

After the filename, the total length of the file will be displayed. Then the file address within BACKUP.001 is displayed. Finally, information about the amount of the file that is available on this disk is shown. In our example the start address is 0, because it is the first file and the entire file is on the disk. If the last file of the disk is incomplete the following message will appear:

```
File incomplete, continue on next disk
```

When all of the available directories and files have been displayed, the program ends. You can insert any other disk from your backup and display the available files.

Explanation

A BACKUP control file consists of a header and individual blocks for directories or files. The header is constructed as follows:

No.	Example	Contents
01	139	Length of header, incl. bytes (139 = $8B)
02-09		8 bytes for the name (BACKUP, filled with spaces)
10	01	Number of disk
11-138	00	unused, contains zeros
139	00	Continue-Flag: 00 = more disks available, 255 (=$FF) = this is the last disk

Information about available directories and files are then added to the header.

Backing up data

Let's begin with the construction of a block, which describes a directory:

No.	Example	Contents
1	70	Length of block including bytes (70 = $46)
2-64		Name of directory (Path)
65/66	09 00	Number of directory entries on disk of this directory (as word Low/High)
67/68	BF 01	Next directory (absolute address), $FF $FF = no more (as word)
69/70	FF FF	FFFF or 0000

Next is the block of the first file. Here is the construction of this block:

No.	Example	Contents
01	34	Length incl. bytes $22
02-13		12 characters for name, not used = \0
14	3	Split-byte (3 = complete, 2 = continue on next disk)
15-18	6F 06 0 0	Length of file (whole) as long integer, i.e. 2 words first low then high, within the words Low/High. In example $0000066F = 1647
19	01	?
20	00	?
21-24	0 0 0 0	Start address in the backup-file (Long integer)
25-28	6F 06 0 0	Length of file on this disk
29	0	Attribute bytes
30	00	?
31-34	5C7D0500	Date and time

After the header there is a block for the directory of the files. This happens even if there were files from the directory on the preceding backup disk. This enables the LISTBACK.BAS program to display the files of any disk.

If all of the files of a directory have been processed as blocks and the disk has more directories, the next block will also be a directory block. RESTORE can distinguish these from file blocks because of the difference in length (70 = directory, 34 = file).

Restoring files without using RESTORE

The problem

The worst thing you can do after losing data is to use a defective disk while restoring the data. Imagine that you have 29 backup diskettes and you call RESTORE. When you are up to the seventh diskette, you are still unable to read the CONTROL file correctly. Then RESTORE aborts and you can't access the files on the remaining diskettes.

The solution

This situation limits the reliability of BACKUP and RESTORE so much that we had to figure out a solution. The following BASIC program, GETBACK.BAS, can restore as many files as needed from backup diskettes. It will start anywhere (for example with the 8th diskette) and you have the choice whether to restore or skip each available file.

However there is one drawback. The program GETBACK.BAS, like the program LISTBACK.BAS, cannot run in GWBASIC. You must use QuickBASIC. If you do not own this BASIC version, ask someone who does own it to compile the program for you. Then you can use the program without QuickBASIC. The companion diskette available for this book contains both the BASIC source code and the QuickBASIC compiled programs.

Backing up data

```
REM getback.bas
REM Program to restore files from BACKUP 3.3
CLS
PRINT "***************************************************************"
PRINT "*     Program to restore files from the BACKUP set   (V3.3)   *"
PRINT "*                      by Manfred Tornsdorf                   *"
PRINT "*             Please do not use the program with APPEND active*"
PRINT "***************************************************************"

DoErrorNr = 0: REM Error number for special routine
FileRest = 0: REM File is not complete, rest of file is missing
FileOpen = 0: REM File is still open for writing
MoreDisk = 0: REM Flag for more disks available = "Y"
Alle = 0: REM Not all files automatically

ON ERROR GOTO Derror
Start:
INPUT "Please input disk number"; DiskNr
IF DiskNr < 1 OR DiskNr > 999 THEN PRINT " Incorrect number (1-999)": GOTO Start

DoNewDisk:
GOSUB GetControlName:
GOSUB TestDiskNummer
OPEN ControlFile$ FOR BINARY AS #1
OPEN BackupFile$ FOR BINARY AS #2
DoDisk:
GOSUB ReadHeader
REM ******************  Read data  ******************
GetBlock:
PRINT
GOSUB GetBlockLen

IF Blocklen = 0 THEN GOTO Diskfinish: REM Check for more disks
IF Blocklen = 70 THEN GOSUB GetDir: GOTO GetBlock: REM Directory
IF Blocklen = 34 THEN
REM File
GOSUB GetDat
IF Alle = 1 THEN In$ = "a": GOTO Automatic
IF FileOpen = 1 THEN In$ = "Y": GOTO Automatic
REM Ask only if no file open for writing
INPUT "Restore file (Y/N) (E = End)(A=All)"; In$
Automatic:
IF In$ = "E" OR In$ = "e" THEN GOTO Ende
IF In$ = "Y" OR In$ = "y" OR In$ = "a" OR In$ = "A" THEN
IF In$ = "A" OR In$ = "a" THEN Alle = 1
GOSUB RestoreFile
END IF: REM Restore file
GOTO GetBlock
END IF: REM File
PRINT "Error, Wrong block lenth:"; Blocklen: CLOSE : END

Diskfinish:
IF MoreDisk = 1 THEN
REM There are more disks
CLOSE #1: REM Control.??? close
CLOSE #2: REM BACKUP.??? close
DiskNr = DiskNr + 1: REM Diskette number increased
BEEP
```

164

Restoring files without using RESTORE

```
            PRINT "Insert next disk Number "; DiskNr; " please."
            PRINT "and press a key to continue."
            WHILE INKEY$ = "": WEND
            GOTO DoNewDisk
            END IF: REM There are more disks

            Ende:
            PRINT "Program end"
            CLOSE
            END

            REM ******************* Sub routines  **************************
            Readit:
            n$ = INPUT$(Num, #1)
            Na = ASC(n$ + CHR$(0))
            RETURN

            GetControlName:
            DiskNr$ = STR$(DiskNr)
            DiskNr$ = MID$(DiskNr$, 2, LEN(DiskNr$) - 1)
            WHILE LEN(DiskNr$) < 3
            DiskNr$ = "0" + DiskNr$
            WEND
            ControlFile$ = "a:\CONTROL." + DiskNr$
            BackupFile$ = "A:\BACKUP." + DiskNr$
            RETURN

            ReadHeader:
            REM ****************** read header of control file **************
            Num = 1: REM read byte length of header
            GOSUB Readit
            PRINT "Length of header  = "; HEX$(Na)
            HeaderLen = Na
            IF HeaderLen <> 139 THEN
            BEEP
            PRINT "Wrong header of Control file":
            CLOSE
            GOTO Ende
            END IF
            Num = 8: REM Read Name
            GOSUB Readit
            PRINT "Name = "; n$
            Num = 1: REM Disk Number read
            GOSUB Readit
            DiskNumber = Na
            PRINT "Diskette number = "; DiskNumber
            IF DiskNumber <> DiskNr THEN
            BEEP
            PRINT "Wrong disk number"
            GOTO DoNewDisk
            END IF
            Num = HeaderLen - 11: REM read remaining headers
            GOSUB Readit
            Num = 1: REM Flag for reading more disks
            GOSUB Readit
            IF Na = 0 THEN MoreDisk = 1
            IF Na = 255 THEN MoreDisk = 0
            PRINT "MoreDisk = "; MoreDisk
```

Quick Tips

In this section we would like to show you several, very interesting tips from many diverse areas that should make your computer work more productive and enjoyable.

Always available - COMMAND.COM

If you don't have a hard disk, you have probably been annoyed when, in certain situations, MS-DOS asks for a disk that contains COMMAND.COM. This usually occurs after you have been working with an application program.

To solve this problem we will define a RAM disk that only contains COMMAND.COM. Also, we use the variable COMSPEC to instruct MS-DOS to get COMMAND.COM from the RAM disk. To define the RAM disk add the following line to your CONFIG.SYS file:

```
DEVICE = VDISK.SYS 40 256 16
```

In order for this line to work, VDISK.SYS must be in the main directory of your BOOT disk and VDISK.SYS must use the drive letter C (VDISK.SYS gives the letter it used after you have switched on your PC). Now add the following lines to your AUTOEXEC.BAT:

```
COPY COMMAND.COM C:\
SET COMSPEC=C:\COMMAND.COM
```

The command interpreter can now be quickly loaded from the RAM disk because it is resident (i.e., always available).

Quick Tips

Tip: Occasionally the drive program for the RAM disk will have a different name, for example RAMDRIVE.SYS.

Concealing executable programs

Sometimes you may now want everyone that works on your computer to be able to use all of the programs available. An easy way to prevent people from using programs is to rename them. MS-DOS will only execute programs that have the endings EXE or COM. If you rename the program FORMAT.COM to FORMAT, you will no longer be able to start it with the original filename.

You need a small batch file, DOCOM.BAT, to start such renamed files. This batch adds the correct ending to the program. For COM files, such as FORMAT.COM, the batch would look like the following batch file If you are using a version of DOS below 3.3, don't use the @ sign in your batch files.

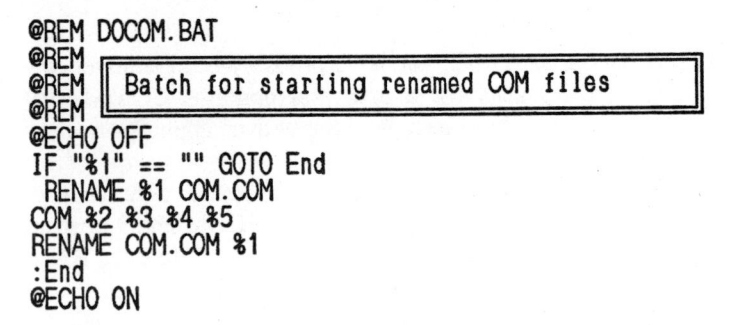

```
@REM DOCOM.BAT
@REM
@REM   Batch for starting renamed COM files
@REM
@ECHO OFF
IF "%1" == "" GOTO End
  RENAME %1 COM.COM
COM %2 %3 %4 %5
RENAME COM.COM %1
:End
@ECHO ON
```

For EXE files you can create the batch, DOEXE.BAT, by renaming the file to EXE.EXE. Call the file with EXE %2 %3 %4 %5.

Tip: This batch will only work if the renamed program is in the current directory. Unlike calling a program, which causes MS-DOS to search all of the directories determined by a path entry, this isn't possible when you rename a program with RENAME.

174

Automatically saving data on a RAM disk

If you have ever created files (e.g., programs) on the RAM disk in order to speed up your work, then you should be able to save your data just as easily so that your work can't be destroyed by a sudden computer failure. The following batch file, SAVED.BAT, saves all of the files on RAM disk D, that aren't in the most current version, to drive A. This makes it easy to save the current version before trying out a new program version:

```
@REM SAVED.BAT
@ECHO OFF
ECHO Securing data of the RAM-disk
ECHO Please insert backup disk
PAUSE
XCOPY D:\*.* A: /m /s
@ECHO ON
```

Tip: Instead of entering D, enter the drive letter of your RAM disk. This will be displayed during the booting process.

The parameter /m instructs XCOPY to copy only the files whose archive flag has been set (file has been changed) and then to erase the flag. The parameter /s processes all of the subdirectories.

To secure only certain files (for example files with the ending .C or .PAS) change the entry D:*.* to D:*.C or to D:*.PAS.

Recovering the hard disk during FORMAT C:

Unlike formatting a disk, formatting a hard disk with FORMAT does not destroy or change data, what is known as a low level format will destroy the data. First FORMAT checks all of the sectors on the hard disk for readability, which is why the heads and cylinders are displayed. The hard disk can be changed only after this is done. Then a new, empty main directory and a corresponding FAT (File Allocation Table) are written on the hard disk.

Quick Tips

As long as FORMAT is still visibly checking the sectors of the hard disk, you can interrupt the formatting process without losing any data (for example, in cases where you didn't want to format). Either use <Ctrl> + <C> or switch off the computer.

Note: Unless you have a good reason, DO NOT try this tip because there are some special DOS versions that instantly destroy the data of the hard disk.

Decreasing the number of files in the main directory

If your main directory is several screen pages long, you can make it more readable by having only two files in this directory: CONFIG.SYS and AUTOEXEC.BAT. Often there are also some other drivers (*.SYS) and COMMAND.COM in the main directory. To change this, use the following procedure:

1. Put all drivers (*.SYS), except for the system file CONFIG.SYS, in the DOS directory. Now you only have to adjust the paths in the CONFIG.SYS. For example if it reads:

   DEVICE=ANSI.SYS

   then change it according to your DOS directory. For example, change it to:

   DEVICE=C:\DOS\ANSI.SYS

   Change these lines for all the other drivers. Now copy the driver programs from the main directory into your DOS directory and erase them from the main directory.

2. You can also transfer COMMAND.COM to the MS-DOS directory. To do this you have to make two changes. First you must add a line to the file CONFIG.SYS:

   SHELL=C:\DOS\COMMAND.COM

   Also you must expand your AUTOEXEC.BAT to include the following line:

```
SET COMSPEC=C:\DOS\COMMAND.COM
```

If necessary, enter the name of your MS-DOS directory instead of \DOS\. Now copy the command interpreter into the MS-DOS directory and erase it from the main directory.

It's possible to transfer COMMAND.COM to a subdirectory because when you are booting, MS-DOS first evaluates the CONFIG.SYS file and then loads the command interpreter (specified by SHELL instruction). The instruction COMSPEC in the AUTOEXEC.BAT ensures that the specified path will also be used later when the command interpreter is being reloaded.

Tip: We have noticed that, when there is a command interpreter in the main directory, occasionally strange effects are produced in MS-DOS when COMSPEC is given a subdirectory. Remove COMMAND.COM from C:\ after backing up your the disk.

Automatically avoiding error messages

Along with the known parameters for calling the command interpreter (/c/p/e), there is a secret parameter (/f), which can be very helpful.

If you call COMMAND.COM with this parameter there will still be an error message and the prompt "Abort, Retry, Failure" in case of diskette error. However, you don't have to press a key because COMMAND.COM will act as though the "F" for "Failure" had been pressed.

You can use this parameter, for example, if you want to copy all of the files from a defective disk but don't want to press a key at every error message.

Since this kind of situation doesn't occur very often, you should create a batch file named FAILRID.BAT and call a command interpreter with the /f parameter before calling a MS-DOS command. Then you can switch back to the original COMMAND.COM. when the batch file is finished

Quick Tips

```
@REM FAILRID.BAT
@REM
@REM   Batch for executing COMMAND.COM without waiting
@REM
@ECHO off
COMMAND /f /c %1 %2 %3 %4 %5
@ECHO on
```

By giving the parameter /f, COMMAND.COM is able to confirm error messages by itself and by entering /c this version of the command interpreter is removed from the memory after processing the given command.

Expanding the PATH

Unfortunately, it is not very easy to expand an existing path. If you enter a directory after PATH, the path will only be valid for that directory. To expand the path you must first look at the previous path by using PATH without a parameter. Enter the path completely and then expand it by using an additional directory.

The following batch should help. Enter it under the name ADDPATH.BAT:

```
@REM ADDPATH.BAT
@REM
@REM   Batch for expanding the path by one directory
@REM
@ECHO off
PATH %PATH%;%1
ECHO New path: %PATH%
@ECHO on
```

Call the batch file and give the directory by which the path should be expanded. Then the new, complete path entry will be displayed. If you only had C:\DOS as a path entry until now and you wanted to add C:BAT, just call ADDPATH with the following line:

ADDPATH C:\BAT

Then you will see the following message:

New Path: C:\DOS; C:\BAT

178

Tip: The next time the computer is switched on, the extended path won't be visible. To make the change permanent, expand the path in the AUTOEXEC.BAT.

Prohibiting FORMAT C: - Protection by LABEL

If you worry about accidentally entering FORMAT C: and then pressing "Y", you can easily protect yourself from doing this if you have DOS 3.2 or higher.

Use LABEL C: to give your hard disk a name. Now, if you mistakenly enter C: instead of A: as the parameter for FORMAT, MS-DOS will ask you to enter the name of the hard disk. If you enter the wrong name or no name, the FORMAT command will end immediately. This additional security question will protect you from accidentally formatting the hard disk.

If you want to prevent other users from giving the correct name for the hard disk, simply choose a name that will be difficult to enter. A good choice would be the blank character with the ASCII value 255. Although this looks like a normal space (ASCII value 32), MS-DOS will not accept a space as the valid character. Here is the procedure for protecting the hard disk (enter <Alt> + <255>, by holding down the <Alt> key and entering the numbers 2,5,5 on the numeric keypad.):

```
LABEL C:
LW<ALT+255>C
```

Now, if someone tries to enter the name of the hard disk during the FORMAT command, he/she will press the space bar after "LW", which will enter the wrong name. This will cause the FORMAT command to abort.

Protecting data from deletion

Certain data shouldn't be easy to delete. Among these are the programs in the MS-DOS directory and other important data.

To make it difficult to change or delete these data you can use the command ATTRIB if you have DOS 3.2 or higher. With ATTRIB you can store, for every file, an attribute (additional information) that will indicate that this file can only be read (READ ONLY).

This will prevent your files from being accidentally deleted. Each time someone tries to access these files, MS-DOS will send the message: "Access denied".

To protect the COMMAND.COM file, in the current directory, simply enter:

```
ATTRIB COMMAND.COM +r
```

To unprotect the file, use the command:

```
ATTRIB COMMAND.COM -r
```

In order to check whether a file is unprotected, call ATTRIB without using the second parameter (+/-r). If an "R" appears before the filename, the file can only be read. Otherwise you can make any changes you want. The ATTRIB command also processes wildcards, so you can use:

```
CD C:\DOS
ATTRIB *.* +r
```

to protect your entire MS-DOS directory from being accidentally deleted.

If you can't remember the ATTRIB command's syntax, then create two new batch files, PROTECT.BAT and UNPROTECT.BAT, so you don't have to enter the command yourself:

```
@REM PROTECT.BAT
@REM
@REM   | Batch for protecting files from being erased |
@REM
@ECHO off
IF "%1" == "" GOTO error
ATTRIB %1 +R
GOTO end:
:error
ECHO Call: file name (Wild cards allowed)
:End
@ECHO on


@REM UNPROTECT.BAT
@REM
@REM   | Batch for releasing erase protection from files |
@REM
@ECHO off
IF "%1" == "" GOTO Error
ATTRIB %1 -R
GOTO End:
:Error
ECHO Call: File name (Wild cards allowed)
:End
@ECHO on
```

"Abort, Retry, Fail?"

You have probably seen the error message "Abort, Retry, Fail" quite often. However, do you know what each one of these options means or when to use them?

Abort   Choose this option if you want to end the current program immediately. This is advisable when an error is both irreparable and unexplainable. For example, suppose you wanted to save an important text on a disk, but receive the "Abort, Retry, Fail" error message when writing the disk. Use "A" to abort and insert another disk.

Retry   This option should be used if the error can be corrected. For example, if you wanted to copy files from the hard disk to drive A

181

Quick Tips

and forgot to insert a disk, you could use this option. Simply insert a disk and select "R".

This option is also valuable if a process should be executed regardless of the circumstances. An example of this would be if you had files that were irreplaceable and wanted to copy them onto a disk. If MS-DOS sends an error message, you should select "R" several times before ending the operation with "A".

Fail This option is useful when you must skip over part of the process of a command but continue executing the rest of the command. If you want to copy many files with COPY *.* but suddenly receive this error message, try "R" (for "Retry") several times and then press "F" to skip the file and continue copying the remaining files.

Occasionally during disk reading operations, "Ignore", will appear:

Ignore Choose this option when there is irreplaceable data and "Retry" doesn't work. MS-DOS won't be able to read certain defective data, but it will continue to read the rest of the file. If you have a large text file, a small part will be destroyed, but the rest will be accurately copied.

You should investigate the cause of such an error message and check whether the data are accurate and/or complete.

"." and ".."

At the beginning of all subdirectories you will find two directories named "." and "..". The directory "." stands for the current directory. So entering DIR . instead of DIR performs the same function.

The directory ".." stands for the next highest directory. This is why the CD.. command switches to the next highest directory. There are also other commands you can use on these two directories. For example:

    COPY   A:

copies the current directory onto drive A just as the longer "COPY *.* A:" does. To quickly erase the current directory you can use the shorter command "DEL ." instead of "DEL *.*". Both perform the same function and are executed after a security prompt. With the command line:

    DIR ..

you can look at the contents of the next highest directory.

Tips on BUFFERS

Even if MS-DOS wants to read only a single byte from a disk or hard disk, a complete sector still has to be read from the volume. This sector is stored into temporary memory buffer. To read another byte from this sector, MS-DOS simply takes it from the buffer. Obviously, with this method, disk access is much faster.

The more buffers MS-DOS can use, the faster you will be able to run certain processes. Use the BUFFERS= command to indicate, in the CONFIG.SYS file, the number of buffers that can be used by MS-DOS. The following setting is appropriate for users with hard disks:

    BUFFERS=20

Test the difference in speed by comparing the time it takes the CHKDSK command to execute after entering the value 2 and then after entering the value 20. Since the CONFIG.SYS is only used when the PC is booted, you must reset the computer, with <Ctrl> + <Alt> + <Del>, each time you change the values. You will notice the time difference immediately.

Do not set the value for BUFFERS too high because each extra buffer requires 512 bytes for data and 20 bytes for the management of the buffer. An increase from 20 to 40 in BUFFERS represents a loss of over 10 kilobytes of memory.

Longer names for directories

As you know, filenames in MS-DOS can only be 8 characters long with a 3 character extension. Many programs even specify certain extensions (BAT, TXT, CHP, etc.); so you can only select the first 8 characters.

However, you can use all 11 characters of a directory name. Directory names can be 11 characters long, except that the period must appear in the name. For example, a directory could have the name DBASE4.DAT (for DBASE4 data) and MS-DOS won't confuse it with DBASE4.PRG. Although using all 11 characters isn't practical in all situations, there are certain times when it can be very useful.

Simple screen output

You would think that the faster a computer is, the easier your work would be. However, this isn't always true. An AT running at 12 megahertz per second and a hard disk will move data over the screen so quickly after the DIR command that you won't be able to read anything, or even stop at the right moment.

While DIR /P offers an easy way to slow down DIR, TYPE is a little more complicated. You could use TYPE I MORE but this is awkward to enter.

Instead, create a batch for all of the MS-DOS commands that display information on the screen too quickly. Then you can use the MORE command, which outputs data page by page. We have already done this for you using the three most important commands. We added the ending "M" to the command names to call attention to MORE. The batch files names are DIRM.BAT, TYPEM.BAT and TREEM.BAT. If you are using a version of DOS below 3.3, don't use the @ sign in your batch files.

Simple screen output

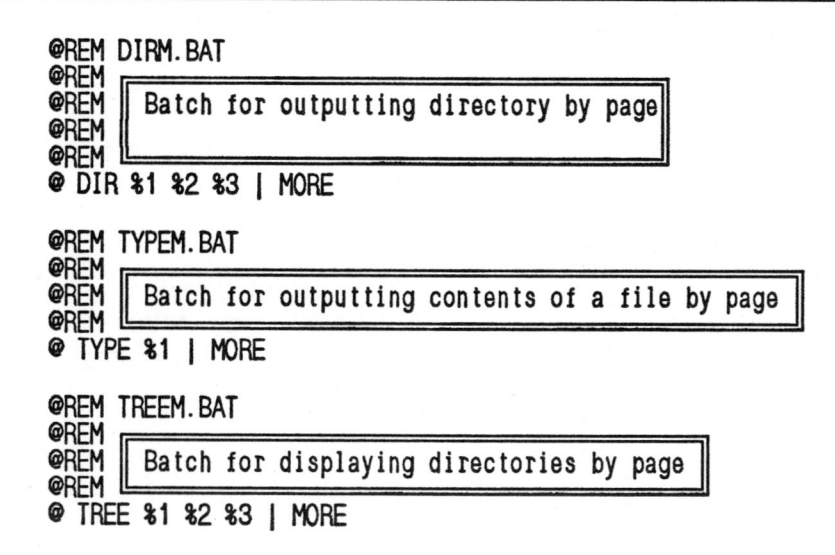

```
@REM DIRM.BAT
@REM
@REM   ┌─────────────────────────────────────────────┐
@REM   │ Batch for outputting directory by page      │
@REM   └─────────────────────────────────────────────┘
@ DIR %1 %2 %3 | MORE

@REM TYPEM.BAT
@REM
@REM   ┌─────────────────────────────────────────────┐
@REM   │ Batch for outputting contents of a file by page │
@REM   └─────────────────────────────────────────────┘
@ TYPE %1 | MORE

@REM TREEM.BAT
@REM
@REM   ┌─────────────────────────────────────────────┐
@REM   │ Batch for displaying directories by page    │
@REM   └─────────────────────────────────────────────┘
@ TREE %1 %2 %3 | MORE
```

GWBASIC programs in the AUTOEXEC.BAT

You can solve many, but not all, problems with MS-DOS and clever batch file programming. Sometimes GWBASIC must be used to solve certain problems.

Call GWBASIC together with a program from a batch file and then use SYSTEM instead of END when it's time to end GWBASIC. Then you can continue to work in the batch file.

This trick can also be used in the AUTOEXEC.BAT. For example, let's assume that for months you have forgotten to do a BACKUP of your hard disk. Then one day you suddenly remember. You need the following BASIC program, BACKDAT.BAS to remind you to do backups:

```
5 REM BACKDAT.BAS
10 REM How long since the last BACKUP ?
20 OPEN "backup.dat" FOR INPUT AS #1
30 LINE INPUT #1,BACK$
40 IF BACK$<>DATE$ THEN GOTO 80
50 BEEP
60 PRINT "You wanted to do a BACKUP today!"
70 WHILE INKEY$ = "": WEND
```

```
80 CLOSE #1
90 SYSTEM
```

Write the date, in the same style GWBASIC uses, for the next BACKUP to a file called backup.dat. Use the following to see the correct date format:

```
? DATE$
```

For our example, this would be "02-14-1990". Use COPY CON BACKUP.DAT to enter the correct date. You can easily create this file by entering:

```
COPY CON C:BACKUP.DAT
02-14-1990<Return>
<CTRL>+<Z><Return>
```

If you then add the line:

```
GWBASIC BACKDAT.BAS
```

to your AUTOEXEC.BAT, the computer will send a warning sound and a message in order to remind you of the necessary BACKUP on the specified day.

Tip: The procedure we just described is not the best procedure, but only an example of how to use GWBASIC in the AUTOEXEC.BAT. If you don't switch on your computer on the day the backup should be performed, the computer will not remind you a few days before or after this date.

In order to do this, you would have to spend much more time in the program to check, for example, whether the current date is lower than or the same as the date in the BACKUP.DAT file.

Rapid disk copying using the hard disk

If you have a PC with a hard disk and only one drive, copying disks can be a time consuming task. If your computer doesn't have enough free memory to copy the disk with only one disk change, you must insert the source and target disks several times. You have to do this when copying an AT disk, regardless of how much data you need to copy.

The following batch file, HDCOPY.BAT, will help if the following requirements are met:

1. The target disk must be already formatted.

2. There can't be any subdirectories on the source disk because they will not be copied.

3. The file "YES" has to be available in the C:\BAT directory. You can easily create this file by entering:

```
COPY CON C:\BAT\YES
Y<Return>
<CTRL>+<Z><Return>
```

For the character sequence <Return>, press the <Enter> key and for <CTRL>+<Z>, press the <Ctrl> and the <Z> keys or the <F6> key.

4. The target diskette should be empty. If not, the files from the source diskette will be copied onto the target diskette as well. The files that are already available will be preserved which means that there may not be enough storage space on the target diskette for your purposes. If you are using a version of DOS below 3.3, don't use the @ sign in your batch files.

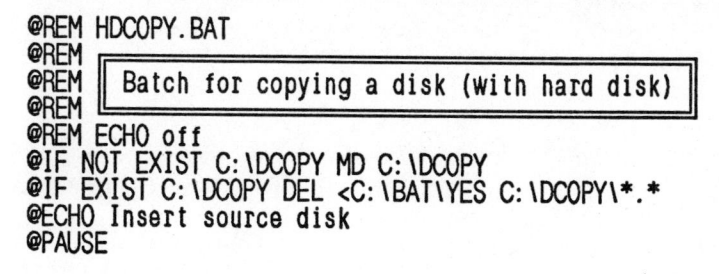

```
@REM HDCOPY.BAT
@REM
@REM   Batch for copying a disk (with hard disk)
@REM
@REM ECHO off
@IF NOT EXIST C:\DCOPY MD C:\DCOPY
@IF EXIST C:\DCOPY DEL <C:\BAT\YES C:\DCOPY\*.*
@ECHO Insert source disk
@PAUSE
```

```
@COPY A:\*.* C:\DCOPY
@ECHO Insert target disk
@PAUSE
@COPY C:\DCOPY\*.* A:
@DEL <C:\BAT\YES C:\DCOPY\*.*
@RD C:\DCOPY
@ECHO Finished
@REM ECHO on
```

Use HDCOPY to call this batch file, then insert the source disk. Press a key and the files from drive A will be copied into the directory C:\DCOPY. After the second call insert the formatted empty target disk, press another key and the files will be copied onto the disk. Then the batch file removes the DCOPY directory.

Tip: An easy way to delete the files from the target disk is to expand the batch file as follows:

```
@ECHO Insert target disk
@ECHO Files in the main directory will be erased!
@PAUSE
@DEL <C:\BAT\YES A:\*.*
```

Intercepting errors with ERRORLEVEL

Obviously it is senseless to continue working with a batch file if there are errors after giving a certain command. After this command, check the system variable ERRORLEVEL in the batch file and, if necessary, end your program.

An example of this would be when you are compiling a machine language program with the MASM, the Microsoft Assembler. You should "link" if MASM was able to compile the source code flawlessly. If you used the following batch file for simplifying the compilation:

```
MASM %1
LINK %1
```

the linker will also be called after an error message from MASM. However, this takes up a lot of time. Instead, use the following batch file for the same purpose:

```
@ECHO OFF
MASM %1
IF ERRORLEVEL 1 GOTO Error
LINK %1
GOTO End
:Error
ECHO Error occurred! Abort process
:End
@ECHO ON
```

Some MS-DOS commands will send an error message to ERRORLEVEL: BACKUP, FORMAT, REPLACE and RESTORE.

Tips on DEL *.*

Be careful when using wildcards while erasing files. There are two situations that could cause data loss:

1. Before entering wildcards after DEL, use DIR to check that you are only deleting the data that should be deleted. Suppose you had the following files in a directory:

   ```
   BOOK1.TXT
   BOOK1.BAK
   BOOK2.TXT
   BOOK2.BAK
   BOOKENT.TXT
   BOOKENT.BAK
   ```

   Now you want to erase these files. Before you enter DEL BOOK*.*, use DIR BOOK*.* to check whether only the corresponding files will be erased. Perhaps the DIR command will also display the files BOOKIDEA.TXT and BOOKCORR.TXT, which shouldn't be deleted. Then you can still save these files.

2. Many times you will want to erase all the data in a directory, for example the data on a disk or in a temporary directory C:\TEMP. Ordinarily you use CD to change to the directory, enter DEL *.* and answer the security prompt with "Y". Be sure that you have chosen the correct directory. Here are two examples of how quickly this process can go wrong:

- The current directory is C:\DOS, and you want to erase all the files in the directory C:\TEMP. By mistake you enter:

  ```
  CD C:\TENP
  DEL *.*
  Y
  ```

  Instead of erasing all the files in the C:\TEMP directory, you have just erased all the files in your MS-DOS directory. This happened because you missed the error message "Invalid directory" and answered "yes" to the security prompt "Are you sure (Y/N)?:".

- The current directory is C:\DBDAT and contains all of your important DBASE data. Now you want to erase the main directory from drive A, so that you can save the changes of the last few days. By mistake you enter:

  ```
  A
  DEL *.*
  Y
  ```

  All of your unsecured DBASE data are lost. "A" causes the error message "Bad command or filename" to be displayed. But it does not change to drive A.

  To protect yourself from this, set up a batch file A.BAT that is always available (PATH) and will change to the correct drive even if you enter "A" instead of "A:". If you are using a version of DOS below 3.3, don't use the @ sign in your batch files.

  ```
  @REM A.BAT
  @ECHO Caution - you have not switched to A.
  @ECHO This will now happen automatically
  @A:
  ```

Protecting AUTOEXEC and CONFIG

Many software packages now contain very simple installation programs. For example, they automatically copy all of the necessary programs into any directory that you indicate, and recognize your computer configuration and install the appropriate programs and options.

However, there are also programs that can cause a lot of trouble for your system files (for example, AUTOEXEC.BAT or CONFIG.SYS). Without your knowledge, FILES can be changed and BUFFERS can be set in the CONFIG.SYS file. Although this can be useful in many instances, you should protect your system files.

The easiest way to do this is by declaring AUTOEXEC.BAT and CONFIG.SYS as *read only* files. If these files were, for example, on a hard disk on drive C, you could do this with the command lines (DOS 3.2 and greater):

```
ATTRIB C:\AUTOEXEC.BAT +R
ATTRIB C:\CONFIG.SYS +R
```

Now these files can't be changed by an installation program without your knowledge. The installation program will display an error message to warn you that they were not changed. Copy your system files into a special backup directory or onto a disk and use:

```
ATTRIB C:\AUTOEXEC.BAT -R
ATTRIB C:\CONFIG.SYS -R
```

to release the protective measure. Examine the change that the installation software requires on the files and make any necessary corrections. One dangerous change could be the additional command:

```
SET COMSPEC=C:\COMMAND.COM
```

because you could be working with different MS-DOS versions with the valid command interpreter in a subdirectory. The additional command could cause error messages and completely stop all further work:

```
COMMAND.COM invalid
```

```
COMMAND.COM cannot be loaded, system ended!
```

Correct such an additional command according to your system requirements to avoid such errors.

Differences between COM, EXE and BAT files

Do you know the differences between these three file types and their functions?

COM COM stands for "compiled" or "command" (i.e., programs that are translated and compiled). This term comes from early computer history when computers had 256 kilobytes. COM files could have a maximum of 64 kilobytes and were subject to various restrictions. The first command always had to be in a segment of the computer memory beginning at address 256 decimal.

EXE EXE stands for "executable". These programs can use the entire MS-DOS memory area and can be located anywhere in the memory. Because of the wider variety of options, they are larger than comparable COM programs with the same functions.

BAT BAT stands for batch files and refers to MS-DOS commands that are stacked together. This term originated when programs were written on punch cards and piles of these cards were processed in batches. Today you can enter such programs with EDLIN and look at them with TYPE.

One very important difference among the three types of files is that they are processed in a certain sequence. After you enter FORMAT, MS-DOS doesn't know whether FORMAT.BAT, FORMAT.EXE or FORMAT.COM should be processed. DOS proceeds in the sequence of COM, EXE, BAT. If you have both FORMAT.COM and FORMAT.BAT in your current directory, the batch file will never be processed but the COM program will always be processed. This leads to two problems, which we will briefly discuss:

1. If you copy a newer version of MS-DOS into your existing MS-DOS directory, old commands could still exist because FORMAT.EXE doesn't replace FORMAT.COM. If you work with the newer version and use the command FORMAT, the new command FORMAT.EXE won't be processed. Instead, the older command FORMAT.COM will be processed. This will result in the error message "Invalid DOS version". Copy the new MS-DOS version into a new directory of your hard disk. Then adapt PATH and COMSPEC to the new version.

2. You can't replace any MS-DOS command in the same directory with a batch file. Even if you have a batch file FORMAT.BAT in your MS-DOS directory along with FORMAT.COM, FORMAT.COM will always be executed first. To call FORMAT.BAT first, copy the batch into a special directory (for example C:\BAT) and give the directory before C:\DOS in the PATH command. The PATH command in the AUTOEXEC.BAT for our example would read:

PATH C:\BAT;C:\DOS

Only then will MS-DOS call the batch file FORMAT.BAT before the command FORMAT.COM.

Counting lines in files

Sometimes you need to know how many lines a text file (for example the source text of a program) contains. The following line demonstrates a simple way to do this:

```
FIND /c " " File name
```

This command line, which searches the given file for a space, does not output each line it finds. At the end it displays the number of lines found. This is done with the /c parameter.

However, this method doesn't always produce the desired result because sometimes a line doesn't contain any spaces. The following batch file COUNT.BAT can help. If you are using a version of DOS below 3.3, don't use the @ sign in your batch files.

```
@REM COUNT.BAT
@REM
@REM   Batch for counting the lines in a file
@REM
@ECHO off
IF "%1" == "" GOTO Error
FIND /c /v "!Dummytext!" %1
GOTO End:
:Error
```

193

```
ECHO Call: File name
:End
@ECHO on
```

This batch counts all the lines, in a given file, that don't contain the text "!Dummy Text!". Obviously, in order for this to work correctly, this text should not appear in your file.

Using commands on all the files in a directory

There are many MS-DOS commands, such as TYPE and FIND, that don't allow the use of wildcards with a filename. However, there is a special command, called FOR DO, for batch programming that can help with this.

For example, to count all of the lines in all of the batch files of a directory use the following line:

```
FOR %a in (*.BAT) DO FIND /c /v "!Dummytext!" %a
```

Now all of the filenames will be displayed with the number of lines for each file. The problem is that it is not only difficult to enter this line but you also have to develop a new line each time you use it. It's a lot easier to use the batch file DO.BAT. This batch file will use any appropriate MS-DOS command on all indicated files. If you are using a version of DOS below 3.3, don't use the @ sign in your batch files.

```
@DO.BAT
@REM
@REM   Batch for using commands on all files
@REM
@ECHO off
IF "%1" == "" GOTO Error
IF "%2" == "" GOTO Error
@FOR %%a IN (%2) DO %1 %%a %3 %4 %5
GOTO End:
:Error
ECHO Call: Command file name <Parameter>
:End
@ECHO on
```

Using commands on all the files in a directory

Before explaining the special abilities of this batch file, we will show you a few applications:

    DO TYPE *.BAT

This displays the contents of all batch files in the current directory one after another.

    DO DEL *.*

This sequentially deletes all the files in the current directory without any confirmation.

Unfortunately, you can't use the batch DO.BAT for the FIND command, even though this MS-DOS command could definitely use wildcards. The reason is that FIND expects the search text before the filename. If we called our batch for FIND in the following format:

    DO FIND "Search text" *.BAT

the filename would be "Search text" and the parameter *.BAT. To use FIND we should write another batch file DOF.BAT, that permits the special requirement of the FIND command:

```
@REM DOF.BAT
@REM
@REM   Batch for using FIND on all files
@REM
@ECHO off
IF "%1" == "" GOTO Error
IF "%2" == "" GOTO Error
IF "%3" == "" GOTO Error
@FOR %%a IN (%3) DO %1 %2 %%a %4 %5
GOTO End:
:Error
ECHO Call: Command filename Parameter
:End
@ECHO on
```

Here is an example to demonstrate how to use this batch. Suppose you wanted to search for the CALL command in all the batch files of the current directory. Simply enter the following command line:

    DOF FIND "CALL" *.BAT

Then all the lines of all the files containing the CALL command will be displayed on the screen. The following is a brief explanation of the most important components of this batch.

After both necessary parameters (MS-DOS command, file specification) have been checked, the actual command line is processed. FOR %%a begins a loop whose variable is called %%a. Use two percentage signs to distinguish this running variable from the replaceable parameters %1 to %9.

By using IN (%3), we specify that all of the files in parentheses should sequentially be assumed by the running variable %%a. Since wildcards are allowed in parentheses, (*.*) causes all the files in the current directory to appear in the running variables.

After DO we indicate the process that should be executed within the loop. You can use %%a and MS-DOS will insert the current filenames. The remainder of the line after the DO command corresponds to the line passed to COMMAND.COM but will be processed for all given files.

We begin by writing the first parameter (the command name %1). Then MS-DOS replaces it with the given command name. Next is the running variable that contains the current filename. Finally we give more parameters with %3 to %5. If you need another parameter for the command after the filename, you can enter it after the file specification.

There is only one small difference in the second batch DOF.BAT. We set the second parameter (search text %2) directly after the command name and use the third parameter %3 in the parentheses to specify the desired files.

Tip: You can also enter the command FOR DO outside of a batch file, directly after the prompt. Then you can use one percentage sign for the running variable %%a, instead of two.

All files on the screen or printer

There is an easy way to display, on the screen or printer, all the files of a directory. You could use DO.BAT, but you would have to use a special batch file for each of the various output devices. Instead, use the COPY command.

For example, to output all the batch files of the current directory onto the screen use the command:

    COPY *.BAT CON

When you are entering data, CON represents the keyboard and when you are displaying data CON represents the screen. To display all of the batch files on the printer, enter:

    COPY *.BAT LPT1

Skipping Prompts

There are many MS-DOS commands, such as DATE and TIME, that wait for a response from the user. The user must react by at least pressing the <Enter> key. Other programs expect either a "Y" or an "N" followed by the <Enter> key. To use these programs in an automatic batch file, you have to simulate the pressing of these keys.

Create three files in your batch directory that will handle this task for you. Change to this directory (for example with CD C:\BAT) and enter the following commands (<RETURN> stands for the <Enter> key, <CTRL>+<Z> for the combination <Ctrl> and <Z> or the <F6> key):

    COPY CON YES
    Y
    <RETURN>
    <CTRL>+<Z><RETURN>

197

```
COPY CON NO
N
<RETURN>
<CTRL>+<Z><RETURN>

COPY CON RETURN
<RETURN>
<CTRL>+<Z><RETURN>
```

Now you have three new files, YES, NO and RETURN, that can help you with your batch file programming.

If you want to write the current system time in a file from a batch file, you only need the following line in your batch file:

```
TIME >TIME.DAT <C:\BAT\RETURN
```

The TIME command writes its screen output in the TIME.DAT file (you can also use a path) and takes its input (the necessary press of the <Enter> key) from the C:\BAT\RETURN file.

To completely erase a batch file from a directory you have to use the DEL *.* command. After the prompt, the command expects you to enter "Y".

To automatically erase a batch file from a directory, take the entry from the C:\BAT\YES file. If the user shouldn't know about the process you can redirect the screen output to the NUL device. This type of line in a batch would look like:

```
DEL <C:\BAT\YES >NUL C:\TEMP\*.*
```

This line automatically erases all of the files in the C:\TEMP directory without leaving any messages on the screen.

Cold Boot from a batch file

Executing a cold boot from a batch file is an excellent way to protect your computer from unauthorized use. If a user enters the wrong password three times, you can reboot the computer from the AUTOEXEC.BAT without any problems.

You need a small machine language program to trigger the cold boot. It's easy to create such a program. Enter the following lines with an editor (for example EDLIN) under the filename BOOT.DEB:

```
A
JMP F000:FFF0

RCX
5
nBOOT.COM
W
Q
```

After storing the file, call the MS-DOS command DEBUG using the following line:

```
DEBUG <BOOT.DEB
```

Now you will have a small executable program, BOOT.COM, that you can call from any batch file. If a user has entered the wrong password several times you can use the following line to reboot the PC:

```
BOOT
```

Calling batch files from batch files (without CALL)

Before MS-DOS Version 3.3, you couldn't call another batch file from a batch file, perform the work in the batch file you called and then return to the original batch file.

With MS-DOS Version 3.3 and above, there is a new command, named CALL. You can use this command to call a different batch file to be used as a subroutine. After you are finished working in the different batch file, MS-DOS will continue in the next command line of the original batch file.

There is no CALL command available in DOS versions before version 3.3. To call another batch file as a subroutine, use the command interpreter COMMAND.COM with the parameter /C and the name of the batch file. By doing this, a new command interpreter will be loaded to process the given batch file.

Quick Tips

To call the batch file BATCH2.BAT from another batch in DOS versions before version 3.3, use the following line:

```
COMMAND /C Batch2.BAT
```

With MS-DOS-version 3.3 and above, you can replace this line with an easier call:

```
CALL Batch2.BAT
```

Here are two batch files that illustrate the procedure for calling a batch file from a batch. The first batch file will be called from the second batch program. If you are using a version of DOS below 3.3, don't use the @ sign in your batch files.

```
@REM TYPEM2.BAT
@REM
@REM  This batch outputs a file by page
@REM
@IF "%1" == "" GOTO Syntax
@IF NOT EXIST %1 GOTO Not_there
@TYPE %1 | MORE
@GOTO End
:Syntax
@ECHO This batch outputs a file by page
@ECHO File name must be given
@GOTO End
:Not_there
@ECHO The file does not exist!!!
:End
```

The following batch file, TYPEALL.BAT, displays on the screen all the given files by page while it calls the first batch TYPEM2.BAT for every appropriate file:

```
@REM TYPEALL.BAT
@REM
@REM  Batch for outputting several files
@REM
@ECHO off
IF "%1" == "" GOTO Syntax
FOR %%a in (%1) do CALL TYPEM2 %%a
GOTO End
:Syntax
ECHO Lists files of the current drive by page
ECHO Call: file name (can contain wildcard)
:End
@ECHO ON
```

Tip: Owners of a MS-DOS version up to and including 3.3 should replace CALL TYPEM with COMMAND /C TYPEM.BAT.

You can pass on other parameters to the called file as shown in the example.

Invalid COMMAND.COM

Have you ever received the following screen message:

```
Invalid COMMAND.COM
Cannot load COMMAND, System halted
```

The command interpreter COMMAND.COM has to be reloaded, but your computer either can't find it or it belongs to another version of MS-DOS. This problem frequently occurs under the following circumstances:

1. You inadvertently assigned the incorrect value to the system variable COMSPEC. Examine all of the system variables with SET and check whether the data for the command interpreter (COMSPEC) is correct. If it isn't correct, change the line SET COMSPEC, in the AUTOEXEC.BAT, to the correct value.

2. You used a different version of MS-DOS but haven't correctly executed the installation of this version. Let's assume you have a version of MS-DOS 3.3 in the directory C:\DOS33 and a version of MS-DOS 4.0 in the directory C:\DOS40. The command interpreter is version 3.3 in the main directory of C:\ and you boot MS-DOS 4.0 from a disk. If you mistakenly set COMSPEC to C:\COMMAND.COM in the AUTOEXEC.BAT of the disk, the stated error message will show up when the command interpreter is reloading.

    If you work with several versions of MS-DOS you should copy the command interpreter into the DOS directory and provide for the correct path to this COMMAND.COM with SHELL in the CONFIG.SYS file and COMSPEC in the AUTOEXEC.BAT file. For an explanation of how this works for a single MS-DOS version, refer to the section on decreasing the number of files in the main directory, found in this chapter. After this you should remove the COMMAND.COM from the main directory.

3. You install a new program and it either makes changes on your system files, AUTOEXEC.BAT and CONFIG.SYS, which changes the data for the

command interpreter or it changes the value for COMSPEC at the start of the program. For example, GEM creates the file GEM.BAT during installation, which in turn, changes COMSPEC. Place a REM in front of this line to prevent the change.

Increasing environment memory (PATH, PROMPT, etc.)

Have you ever received the following error message, for example, after the SET command:

```
Out of environment space
```

MS-DOS adapts to its environment by using system variables, which are filed in the environment memory. The most important system variables are:

PATH	Contains all of the path data.
PROMPT	Contains the system prompt.
COMSPEC	Contains the path and name of the command interpreter.

When you are expanding a system variable (for example extending the path), it's possible that the memory reserved for the environment by MS-DOS is no longer sufficient. If this is the case, the above error message will appear.

In order to obtain a larger system environment, call a new COMMAND.COM with the parameters /P /E:1000. /P indicates that the command interpreter should load permanently and replace the existing command interpreter, /E indicates that the size of the environmental memory should be set to the given value (in bytes).

Caution: If you call the operating system from a program (for example from WORD with "ESC L R " or from WORKS with "ALT F R") and call a new COMMAND.COM as described, you won't be able to return to the application program (WORD, WORKS etc.). All of the data that hasn't been saved will be lost.

This is why you should permanently increase the environmental memory by using the SHELL command in the CONFIG.SYS file. If your COMMAND.COM is in the subdirectory C:\DOS and you want to permanently set the size of the environmental memory to 1000 bytes, add the following line to your CONFIG.SYS file:

```
SHELL=C:\DOS\COMMAND.COM /P /E:1000
```

Note: The size of the environment is set to 160 bytes in DOS 3.2.

Optimum use of the current directory

As you know, MS-DOS applies all commands, that have an effect on files, to the current directory, if no path has been given. If you use CD C:\TEMP to select the TEMP directory of the hard disk and enter DEL *.*, all of the given files in the current directory will be deleted.

However, MS-DOS also remembers the current directory of every disk drive, which can be very helpful. Suppose you have a disk drive A and a hard disk C. You could, for example, make the subdirectory A:\DOS of drive A the current directory with:

```
A:
CD A:\DOS
```

Then you could change to drive C and make C:\TEMP the current directory:

```
C:
CD C:\TEMP
```

However, the current directory for drive A won't be lost. You can easily confirm this by switching to drive A and requesting the current directory with CD:

```
A:
CD
```

By using the current directories of different drives, you don't have to enter the paths yourself. For example, to sequentially copy all of the COM and EXE files from the current directories A:\DOS to C:\TEMP, you only need to use the following command lines:

Quick Tips

```
COPY A:*.COM C:
COPY A:*.EXE C:
```

By entering the drive letter with the colon you refer to the current directory of this drive. If you want to look at the main directory of drive A, you must enter the backslash after the colon:

```
DIR A:\
```

BACKUP & XCOPY tips

You can backup files, directories or the contents of an entire volume with the MS-DOS command BACKUP and retrieve the data with RESTORE. Here are some examples:

```
BACKUP C:\DOS\*.* A:
```

This backs up all the files in the C:\DOS directory:

```
BACKUP C:\DOS\*.* A: /S
```

All the files in the C:\DOS directory as well as all of the subdirectories contained within this directory are backed up.

```
BACKUP C:\*.* A: /S
```

This backs up the entire hard disk with all of the subdirectories on drive A.

Many people don't know that you can also use BACKUP to backup as many files as you want from all of the directories. For example, if you have important text files with the ending ".TXT" in different directories of the hard disk and want to backup them with BACKUP, simply enter the following line:

```
BACKUP C:\*.TXT A: /S
```

This command will backup all of the text files with the given extension from any and all directories. You could also use this trick to backup all of the C sources from the subdirectories C:\MSC\SOURCE and C:\QC\SOURCE with one command:

BACKUP C:*.C A: /S

This trick also works with the XCOPY command. This command only allows you to copy as many files as will fit on a single disk, you have direct access to these files anytime and can copy them with the regular MS-DOS command COPY. If you tried this with BACKUP it would be either completely impossible or possible on a limited basis, depending on the MS-DOS version. The command line for XCOPY reads:

XCOPY C:*.C A: /S

To take full advantage of BACKUP and XCOPY you should ensure that the filenames follow a certain pattern. While this automatically applies to texts and C programs, Multiplan files are different. You can give your Multiplan charts whatever names you like, for example TAX, TAX.WK1, TAX.MUL or TAX.CHA.

You should use a uniform ending for charts, for example ".CHA", so that you can backup these files from different directories at the same time.

If you have different kinds of files (texts, databases, diagrams) that are part of the same project, use a pattern for these filenames. For example, you could have all files concerning annual income taxes begin with T_. Here is an example:

Texts	T_??????.TXT (for WORD)
Databases	T_??????.DBF (for DBASE)
Charts	T_??????.CHA (for Multiplan)
Diagrams	T_??????.PCX (for PC Paintbrush)

To backup all of the files that you will use to figure your taxes, simply enter:

BACKUP C:\T_*.* A: /S

A DOS Prompt with Time, Date and Path

Some MS-DOS users like to have as much information on the screen as possible and others prefer as little as possible. If you belong to the first category, you can

Quick Tips

have the prompt display the time, date and current path. The following command line makes this possible:

    PROMPT $t $d pg

The $t displays the time, $d displays the date and $p is for the drive and path. The $g is for the character ">". However, this command will make the prompt line very long and difficult to view. Try it out and see for yourself.

We have a better solution: Transfer these data to the first line of the screen and output the information there in inverse video. The following batch TOPLINE.BAT will do this for you:

```
@REM TOPLINE.BAT
@REM
@REM  | Prompt with time, date and path (with ANSI.SYS) |
@REM
@PROMPT $e[s$e[f$e[7mTime $t$h$h$h$h$h$h $d $p$g$e[K$e[u$e[Om$p$g
```

To remove the top line simply enter your usual prompt:

    PROMPT PG

```
Time 15:53 Fri  1-26-1990 C:\>
C:\>
```

Fig.. 12: The top line displaying the time and date

A DOS Prompt with Time, Date and Path

In order for this batch to work, you must have the screen driver ANSI.SYS linked to your CONFIG.SYS. Use the following line in the CONFIG.SYS if your ANSI.SYS driver is located in the DOS directory of drive C.:

DEVICE=C:\DOS\ANSI.SYS

For C:\DOS enter your MS-DOS directory of the hard disk that contains the ANSI.SYS file or be sure that ANSI.SYS is available on your boot disk and use the line:

DEVICE=ANSI.SYS

Those who would like to adapt the top line to their own needs might be interested in the functions of the various commands:

$e[The Esc command for the screen driver ANSI.SYS. $e is changed into the code for ESC.

$e[s   Saves the current position of the cursor.

$e[f   Sets the cursor to the specified position ($e[10;20f e.g. to line 10 and column 20). If, as in our case, no position is indicated, the cursor will go to the upper left corner.

$e[7m   Causes all of the subsequent screen output to appear inverted.

$t   Displays the current system time.

$h   Functions like the BACKSPACE key (i.e. moves the cursor back one or more spaces). By displaying $h several times, the seconds and hundredths of a second are overwritten.

$d   Prints the current system date.

pg   Prints the drive and path and the character ">".

$e[K   Deletes the rest of the line.

$e[u   Sends the cursor back to the initial saved position.

$e[0m   Cancels the inverted display of screen output.

pg   Prints the drive and path in the current line as a prompt.

Quick Tips

If you receive the error message "Out of environment space", refer to the section on increasing the system environment found in this chapter.

Exchanging data with an AT and an XT

Before we discuss passing data from AT to XT, you should know that only 360Kb disks can be used to exchange data between AT and XT on 5 1/4" drives. It isn't possible for a 360Kb drive to read or write the 1.2Mb disks.

Many 360Kb drives either can't read an AT written 360Kb disk or can only read one occasionally. Whether or not this happens seems to depend on chance or how important the data is. You can use a simple trick to get around this problem.

When transferring data from AT to XT, only use disks that have been written by AT. This might sound like a contradiction but it almost always works. Here is the procedure for transferring data:

1. Take a completely unformatted 360Kb disk and format it on AT with:

   FORMAT A: /4

2. Copy the data you want transferred from AT onto the disk.

3. Copy the data onto XT as usual. Do not write any data from the XT on the transfer disk.

The reason why this trick works is that the read/write head of the AT drive can write 80 tracks per side while the read/write head of a 360Kb drive can only write 40 tracks. This means that the magnetized track of an AT drive is more narrow than the magnetized track of an XT drive. If an XT writes one track of a disk and the AT then writes its data on such a track, there will be "magnetized remains", which cause reading errors

If a disk has only been written by an AT then there won't be any "magnetized remains" and there won't be any reading errors. Transferring data from the other direction (XT writes, AT reads) always works with properly functioning devices.

Finding traces of old MS-DOS versions

Have you ever installed a newer version of a program onto your hard disk but when you called the program the old version started up instead? This happened to us once after installing a new compiler version. The compiler had a new version 5.0 of the linker, but every time we called the compiler the old version 3.05 would start.

This happened because the MS-DOS directory had the old version of LINK.EXE while the directory of the compiler had the new version. We added this directory to the existing PATH. The MS-DOS commands directory, with the old version, came before the compiler directory in the PATH command, so MS-DOS found the old version first and started it up.

If something similar happens to you, use PATH to see which directories are searched for executable programs and note the sequence. Then check the directories for older versions.

Another cause is the various endings that executable programs can have: COM, EXE or BAT. Some users install new versions of MS-DOS by simply copying all of the disks into the existing directory. They believe that by doing that they are overwriting all of the old versions.

However, this is only true if both the old and new commands have exactly the same filenames. Here are two examples that demonstrate why that isn't always the case:

1. Until MS-DOS version 3.3, the command for adapting the keyboard to different countries' languages was KEYB??.COM. Germany, for example, was KEYBGR.COM. Beginning with MS-DOS version 3.3 the command changed to KEYB.COM and you had to add the GR as a parameter. So if you copied all the MS-DOS disks of version 3.3 into a directory that contained an older version, it would not overwrite KEYBGR.COM.

2. Some of the commands changed endings from COM to EXE in the new versions (for example FDISK). If you copied a new DOS version with FDISK.EXE into the directory of an older DOS version with FDISK.COM, the new command would not replace the old one. Since MS-DOS looks in a directory for a COM file first and then looks for an EXE file, the older COM version will always start first.

Quick Tips

So if you want to install a newer version of MS-DOS you should use either a new, empty directory and change the specifications for PATH, COMSPEC and SHELL accordingly, or backup the old DOS directory by copying it onto backup disks, erase it from the hard disk and copy the new DOS commands.

You can also use our batch file WHEREFILE.BAT, from the section on searching for files, to find different versions of a program on the hard disk. For example, to find all of the versions of FDISK.COM and FDISK.EXE, simply enter:

```
WHEREFILE FDISK
```

Tip: Remember that when you are searching for files with WHEREFILE.BAT that the filenames have to be entered in uppercase letters and that wildcards are not permitted. Instead of *.txt, use .TXT.

40Mb hard disks - Saving data easily

Do you have a hard disk with more than 32Mb capacity for an MS-DOS version 3.3 or above? Your hard disk was probably divided into two or more partitions with FDISK. If you don't have any useful application for the second partition D, then you could use the second partition to save backup data.

With a 40Mb hard disk you have more than 8 megabytes available, so you can backup data faster than ever before. For example, to secure all of the texts, with the ending .TXT, onto partition D, use the following command line:

```
BACKUP C:\*.TXT D: /S
```

The BACKUP command automatically sets up the directory D:\BACKUP and stores the files in this directory. This method is so fast that you won't want to do without it.

Tip: This method of backing up data cannot completely replace saving data on a disk, since data saved in drive D would be useless if the hard disk or the partition data (FDISK) were destroyed. Also, using FORMAT C: or DEL *.* on drive C can't damage the data in drive D.

Securing AT system data

If your AT with a hard disk is working perfectly, keep it that way by making a note of the displayed data of SETUP. The specifications of your hard disk are especially important. The AT stores the most important hardware information (screen display, drives, hard disks, etc.) in a memory area that runs on a battery after you switch off the computer.

One time our battery expired and the data in this storage area was deleted. The next time we switched on the computer it displayed an error message and required us to call the SETUP program using a special key combination and reset the values.

Resetting the date, time and disk drives weren't a problem, but we could only use the numbers 1-41 to set the type of hard disk. Since this caused us much anxiety, we now keep a sheet, taped to the side of the computer, that contains all of the important data of the SETUP program. We have had to re-enter information about the hardware a few times since then, but a quick glance at the sheet on the side of the computer made the task much easier.

Tip: Usually the screen will tell you how to get to SETUP after you have turned on the AT (for example "Press (DEL) to run SETUP"). Otherwise you can look it up in your AT manual.

Accessing the main directory with one key press

To get to the the main directory from any subdirectory use the command:

CD \

Instead of entering the backslash, you could create a batch file, C.BAT, which contains this command line. Now you can quickly switch to the main directory.

211

Quick Tips

Protecting the screen with SCREEN.BAS

There are times when you want to interrupt your work on the computer without switching it off. The screen display won't change at all during this time, so you run the risk of "burning in" the contents on the screen (i.e. the contents would stay visible). There are many ways to eliminate this problem. An easy, practical way to do this is with the following BASIC program, SCREEN.BAS. This program erases the screen and then switches it back on at the press of a key.

```
5 REM SCREEN.BAS
10 REM Turn off screen
20 CLS
30 WHILE INKEY$ = "": WEND
40 SYSTEM
```

To interrupt your work on the computer for a short time simply call this program with:

```
GWBASIC SCREEN.BAS
```

To continue working just press a key, for example, the space bar. It's even easier if you write the call to GWBASIC and the given program in a SCREEN.BAT batch file.

Aborting after incorrectly changing drives

If you have ever mistakenly entered A: when there was no disk in drive A, MS-DOS will give you an error message and ask:

```
Abort, Retry, Fail?
```

You can press A for abort or R for retry as often as you want, without inserting a formatted disk, but you can only get out of this situation by pressing "F" for "Fail". Then the following error message will appear:

```
The current drive is no longer valid! >
```

After the ">" character you can specify the new drive, for example C:, and change to it by pressing the <Enter> key.

Quickly deleting a command line

Sometimes after entering a long MS-DOS command, you decide that you don't want to execute the command. Using <Backspace> to delete all of the characters on the line can be time consuming. It's much easier to press the <ESC> key. A backslash will appear at the end of the written line and the cursor will jump to the next free line. Now you can enter a new command.

About the Authors

A while ago we received a letter from one of our readers, who, in addition to making suggestions and giving advice, asked about the authors. Since then, we have learned that there is, in the computer world, an understandable interest in the human side of hardware, software and books. So the following is our "story".

Step one: The problems of a beginner

It all started a few years ago when I decided to switch from the legendary home computer, the Commodore C64, to a PC for my daily work.

It was like starting all over again - the feeling that you didn't know anything, breakdowns and trouble after every small success, etc. The most depressing part was the manuals, which were full of information, but were not written for beginners. I received most of my help from the people who, in person and over the phone, patiently helped me through the worst. My "little brother" also came to my aid, contributing a lot more perseverance and enthusiasm to problem solving than I did.

Step two: You don't have to do everything by yourself!

The second step was to do something about the existing literature. I wrote my own book for beginners, **MS-DOS for Beginners**, which could have been subtitled, "For Beginners by a Beginner". There were two advantages in writing the book: 1) I really learned MS-DOS and 2) I could use my experiences with problems to help the reader avoid the same problems.

The hard drive presented many problems for me, but thankfully, my brother helped me by providing the information I needed. Obviously, the physics he studied proved very useful.

Quick Tips

Step three: The principle of division of labor

From that time on I knew that there would be other books. I struggled with the question of what the user most wanted and then planned what I would do.

It helped that I, as a teacher, was confronted daily with "beginners" and their problems. The fact that my subjects (German and History) had almost nothing in common with computers was actually to my advantage. I didn't have to worry about writing a book just for mathematicians and computer operators.

With his extensive knowledge of the operating system, my brother helped me with the mysteries of programming. His detailed explanations helped me find solutions to the problems I was facing.

In this way we have written two beginners books on MS-DOS, two books on BASIC and three books on WORD. We were happy to hear that our readers were receptive to our combination of technical know-how and user-friendly language.

Step four: Cooperation with the reader

Our readers' letters were important because they forced us to stick to the needs and wants of the user. We will continue to try to write informative and better books. Thank you very much!

H. Tornsdorf

Index

%%a 195
%PROMPT% 108
"." 182
".." 182
/a 119
/c 193
/COLOR 144
/DOS 144
/E 202
/EXIT 143
/f 150, 177
/L 153
/m 149, 175
/MAINT 144
/MENU 143
/n 152
/P 202
/PROMPT 143
/s 150, 175
<DIR> 94
<Num Lock> 113
@ character 8
_PARK.COM 84

A.BAT 190
Abort 181
Add 134, 137, 140
ADDPATH.BAT 178
ANSI.SYS 103, 107
APPEND 169
Archive Flag 149

ASCII code 44
ASK.EXE 33
AT 132
ATTRIB 91, 180
attribute byte 104
AUTOEXEC.BAT 2, 11, 32, 66

BACKDAT.BAS 185
backslash 115
BACKUP5, 54,126, 150, 157, 204, 210
backup copies 75
BACKUP.LOG 153
BAK 147
BASIC 72
BASIC compilers 21
BAT 192
batch files 1, 192, 198
BATCH2.BAT 199
BOLD.BAT 105
BOLD.DAT 118
BOOT.COM 198
BOOT.DEB 198
BS.BAT 116
BUFFERS= 183

C.BAT 211
cache programs 128
CALL 15, 140, 195, 199
Change 136, 137, 140
Change Colors 134

Index

character attribute 104
CHKDSK 30, 62, 69
CHR$() 99
CLS 104
cold boot 198
COM 7, 174, 191
COMMAND /C 15
Command interpreter 127, 138
Command Prompt 134, 136
COMMAND.COM...173, 177, 199, 202
commands 2
compiler 22
COMSPEC..27, 73, 177, 192, 200, 202
CON 117, 196
CONFIG.SYS 11, 176
control file 161
COPY 149, 196
COUNT.BAT 193
current directory 182

DATE 2, 80
DEBUG 23, 35, 82, 114, 198
DEL *.* 147, 197
DIR 48, 189
DIRM.BAT 184
DISKCOPY 123
DO 196
DO.BAT 194
DOALL!!!.BAT 69
DOCOM.BAT 174
DOEXE.BAT 174
DOF.BAT 196
DOS utility programs 138
DOSSHELL 137
DOSSHELL.BAT 133, 134, 144
DOSSHELL.OLD 133
DOSUTIL 137

ECHO 8
ECHO OFF 8
EDLIN 7, 192
END.BAT 84

environment variables 108, 109
environmental memory 201
error message 21
ERRORLEVEL 35, 188
ESC 213
ESC.DAT 118
escape code 115
escape sequences 104
EXE 7, 174, 191
EXE2BIN 129
expanded memory 131
extended keys 116

Fail 182
FDISK 210
File System 134
file named PW.BAT 86
FIND 50, 53, 62, 63, 73, 194, 195
FINDALL.BAT 65
FINDMORE.BAT 71
FINDTEXT.BAT 154
FOR %%a 195
FOR ... . DO 11
FOR DO 194, 196
FORMAT 38, 126, 175, 179
FORMAT C 147

GETBACK.BAS 158, 163
GOTO 12
GROUP 137
GWBASIC........................... 18, 65, 85

HDCOPY 187
HDCOPY.BAT 186
help screens 37, 42
HELP.BAT 42
HIDE 94
HIDE.COM 89

218

Index

IF 12
Ignore 182
IN (%2) 195
INPUT.COM 83
INPUT.DEB 82
INSERT 136
INSTALL 125
interpreter 21
inverse video 109

KEYDEF.BAT 120

LABEL C 179
LINK.EXE 208
LISTBACK.BAS 157, 158
LPT1 98
LPT2 98

machine language 23
main group 134
MEU 142
MODE 95, 97, 131
MORE 63, 184

NO_BS.BAT 116
normal keys 116
NORMAL.BAT 105
Norton Utilities 156
NUL device 43, 81
NUMBYTE.BAS 54
NUMLOCK.COM 114
NUMLOCK.DEB 113

OLDKEY.BAT 120

parameters 4, 13, 15, 26
PARK 84
PARK.BAT 84
PARK.COM 84
pass parameters 10
Passwords 141
PATH 16, 27, 39, 192, 202, 208
PAUSE 9, 63

PC TOOLS 156
PCIBMDRV.MOS 133
PCMSDRV.MOS 133
PCMSPDRV.MOS 133
pipe character 3
PRINT MARGIN BORDER 96
Program 136
PROMPT 26, 29, 202
    $d 205, 207
    $e[..................................... 206
    $e[0m 207
    $e[7m 206
    $e[f 206
    $e[K 207
    $e[s 206
    $e[u 207
    $g 205
    $h 207
    $p 205
    pg 207
    $t 207
PROTECT.BAT 180, 181
PRTDAT.BAS 117, 118

QUICKBASIC 22, 86

RAM DISK 3
RAMDRIVE.SYS 174
READ ONLY 180, 190
RECOVER 148, 155
redirection character 16, 30
REM 9
resident 174
RESTORE 126, 151, 203
RestoreFile 170
Retry 181

SAVED.BAT 175
screen attributes 103
SCREEN.BAS 211
search 61
SELECT program 131
SET 26, 28, 107, 108, 200

219

Index

SETUP 210
SHEL.MEU 142
SHELL 68, 70 201, 202
SHIFT 14
SORT 3, 49
SORTFILE.BAS 77
sorting 50
sorting by date 52
sorting by time 52
source disk 187
special characters 15
SYS 90, 126
SYSTEM 69, 185
system variables 201

target disk 186
TIME, ... 2, 80
TIME.DAT 197
TIME.OLD 80
TOPLINE.BAT 205
TREE 56, 57, 59
TREEM.BAT 184
TXTSHELL 135
TXTSHELL.MEU 134
TYPE 133, 143, 192, 194
TYPEALL.BAT 200
TYPEM.BAT 184
TYPEM2.BAT 200

UNPROTECT.BAT 80, 181
USER.LOG 83, 85
USER.OLD 83, 85

VDISK.SYS 173
View File 142

warm boot 127
WHEREDIR.BAT 57
WHEREFILE.BAT 209
WHERFILE.BAT 61
wildcards 189

XCOPY 149, 204

220

Companion Disk

For your convenience, the batch files and BASIC programs described in this book are available on a 5-1/4" 360K IBM format floppy diskette. You should order the companion disk if you want the programs, but don't want to type them in from the listings in the book.

All programs on the disk have been fully tested. You can change the programs to suit your particular needs. The companion disk is available for $14.95 + $2.00 for postage and handling within the U.S.A. ($5.00 for foreign orders).

When ordering, please give your name and shipping address. Enclose a chec' money order or credit card information. Mail your order to:

Abacus

5370 52nd Street S.E • Grand Rapids, MI 49512

Or for fast service call **616/698-0330**

For orders only call **1-800-451-4319**

Abacus pc catalog

Order Toll Free 1-800-451-4319

5370 52nd Street SE • Grand Rapids, MI 49512
Phone: (616) 698-0330 • Fax: (616) 698-0325

Beginners Books for new PC Users

Beginners Series books remove the confusing jargon and get you up and running quickly with your PC.

PC and Compatible Computers for Beginners - For the absolute newcomer to personal computers. Describes the PC and all of its components in an non-technical way. Introduces DOS commands.
ISBN 1-55755-060-3　　　　　　　　$18.95
Canada: 52072 $22.95

MS-DOS for Beginners - Describes the most important DOS commands clearly and understandably. Teaches skills required to more effectively use your PC.
ISBN 1-55755-061-1　　　　　　　　$18.95
Canada: 52071 $22.95

Excel for Beginners - Newcomers to this powerful spreadsheet and graphics software will learn to master Excel's many features in a short while. Dec. '90
ISBN 1-55755-067-0　　　　　　　　$18.95
Canada: 52067 $22.95

Microsoft Works for Beginners - A thorough introduction to this "all-in-one" software package. Loaded with simple, practical examples.
ISBN 1-55755-063-8　　　　　　　　$18.95
Canada: 52070 $22.95

Ventura Publisher for Beginners* - Presents the basics of the premier desktop publishing package. Many examples and illustrations.
ISBN 1-55755-064-6　　　　　　　　$18.95
Canada: 52074 $22.95

To order direct call Toll Free 1-800-451-4319

In US and Canada add $4.00 shipping and handling. Foreign orders add $12.00 per item. Michigan residents add 4% sales tax

Beginners Books for new PC Users

Unix for Beginners - Clearly describes this popular operating system, Logon procedures, file concepts and commands using simple and clear examples.
ISBN 1-55755-065-4 $18.95
Canada: 52073 $22.95

Lotus 1-2-3 for Beginners - Presents the basics with examples that are presented clearly and without confusing 'computer jargon'. Includes Release 2.2 information.
ISBN 1-55755-066-2 $18.95
Canada: 52069 $22.95

GW-BASIC Programming for Beginners* - A simple introduction to programming the PC using the BASIC language. Learn many of the commands writing sample programs and taking chapter quizzes.
ISBN 1-55755-062-X $18.95
Canada: 52068 $22.95

Microsoft Word for Beginners - Explains what a beginner needs to know to become more productive with this powerful word processor Step-by-step examples.
ISBN 1-55755-068-9 $18.95
Canada: 52075 $22.95

COBOL for Beginners* - Teaches this popular language using MBP, MicroFocus and Microsoft COBOL. Includes quizzes, explana-tions and demonstrations. Jan. '90
ISBN 1-55755-070-0 $18.95 *NEW*
Canada: 53904 $22.95

dBASE IV for Beginners - Simply and easily explains the fundamentals of dBASE. Learn to operate this package in no time and utilize it's powerful commands and functions. Jan. '90
ISBN 1-55755-069-7 $18.95
Canada: 52066 $22.95

To order direct call Toll Free 1-800-451-4319
In US and Canada add $4.00 shipping and handling. Foreign orders add $12.00 per item. Michigan residents add 4% sales tax

Developers Series Books

Developers Series books are for the professional software developer that requires in-depth technical information and programming techniques.

PC System Programming for Developers a literal encyclopedia of technical and programming information. Features parallel working examples in MS-DOS, Pascal, C, ML. Topics include: memory layout, DOS operations and interrupts from ML and high level languages, using extended and expanded memory, device drivers (incl. CD-ROMs), hard disk partitions, PC ports, mouse driver programming, COM and EXE programs, fundamentals of BIOS, programming graphics and sound, TSR programs, complete appendices and more. 
ISBN 1-55755-035-2 $39.95
Canada: 52092 $51.95
Book/disk combination
ISBN 1-55755-036-0 $59.95
Canada: 52444 $74.95

PC File Formats and Conversions for Developers describes in detail file formats for major software applications. Learn how to transfer files from one PC application to another. This book/disk combination includes file conversion software. Feb. '90.
Includes companion diskette
ISBN 1-55755-059-X $34.95
Canada: 53906 $45.95

Turbo Pascal Internals for Developers describes programming tips and techniques using the best-selling Pascal programming language today. March '90. Includes two companion diskettes.
ISBN 1-55755-080-8 $49.95
Canada: 53910 $64.95

More Titles Coming Soon!

To order direct call Toll Free 1-800-451-4319
In US and Canada add $4.00 shipping and handling. Foreign orders add $12.00 per item. Michigan residents add 4% sales tax

Productivity Series Books

Productivity Series books are for the user who wants to become more productive sooner with their PC.

Printer Tips & Tricks describes how printers work, basic printer configurations using DIP switches, using MS-DOS commands for simple printer control and includes utilities on a 5 1/4" companion diskette to demonstrate the most popular software commands. Useful printer accessories, font editor, and printing tricks and tips. Dec. '89.
Includes companion diskette.
ISBN 1-55755-075-1 $34.95
Canada: 53903 $45.95

MS-DOS Tips & Tricks contains dozens of tips from the pros on using MS-DOS. Describes tricks and tips on finding any file on hard disk, copying data from a backup without the RESTORE commands, protecting your data, cold-starting your PC from a batch file and more. Feb. '90.
ISBN 1-55755-078-6 $17.95
Canada: 53907 $23.95

PC Tools Complete is a complete reference to the PC Tools software, the best-selling softare utility for years. It thoroughly covers all of the many features of each of the utilities that make up this all-encompassing software package. Jan. '90
ISBN 1-55755-076-X $22.95
Canada: 53905 $29.95

Complete Guide to the Atari Portfolio contains valuable information about the Atari Portfolio, the smallest PC available on the market. Designed for both the beginner and experienced PC user it covers hardware, software, built-in applications, printing and transferring data to other computers and much more.
ISBN 1-55755-058-1 $17.95
Canada: 53900 $23.95

More Titles Coming Soon!

To order direct call Toll Free 1-800-451-4319
In US and Canada add $4.00 shipping and handling. Foreign orders add $12.00 per item. Michigan residents add 4% sales tax

Quick Reference Books

Quick Reference Series books are convenient, durable books made to last. You'll find clear, concise information quickly at your fingertips.

MS-DOS Versions **3.3 & 4.0**
ISBN 1-55755-000-X $9.95
Canada: 52079 $12.95

Lotus 1-2-3 Versions **2.2 & 3.0**
ISBN 1-55755-014-X $9.95
Canada: 52076 $12.95
Available Dec. '89

WordPerfect
Covers Versions **5.0 & 5.1**
ISBN 1-55755-015-8 $9.95
Canada: 52085 $12.95
Available Jan. '90

Multiplan
ISBN 1-55755-002-6 $9.95
Canada: 52080 $12.95

GW-BASIC
ISBN 1-55755-001-8 $9.95
Canada: 52078 $12.95

dBASE III Plus & IV
ISBN 1-55755-013-1 $9.95
Canada: 52077 $12.95
Available Dec. '89

PC Tools Companion
All the information you require for working with best-selling PC tools software. Features a durable hardback cover that makes the book perfect for laptop users.
ISBN 1-55755-012-3 $12.95
Canada: 53908 $16.95
Available Jan. '90

UNIX/ XENIX Reference Guide - Gain quick access to vital information on UNIX and XENIX. Commands listed with syntax, options, examples of use and reference to other commands.
Soft cover.
ISBN 1-55755-031-X $12.95
Canada: 52083 $16.95

To order direct call Toll Free 1-800-451-4319
In US and Canada add $4.00 shipping and handling. Foreign orders add $12.00 per item. Michigan residents add 4% sales tax

More PC Books

Computer Viruses - A High-Tech Disease describes the relatively new phenomena among personal computer users, one that has the potential to destroy large amounts of data stored in PC systems. Simply put, this book explains what a virus is, how it works and what can be done to protect your PC against destruction.
ISBN 1-55755-043-3　　　　　　$18.95
Canada: 52089 $24.95

Science & Engineering Applications on the IBM/PC* - Covers applications from diverse fields, including astronomy, biology, chem-istry, physics, mathematics and others. Includes program listings in PC BASIC and GW-BASIC. 260 pp
ISBN 0-916439-65-8　　　　　　$19.95
Canada: 52087 $25.95

Turbo Pascal Tricks & Tips* Topics covered: sort routines, binary trees, B-trees, balanced trees, MS-DOS screen output routines, time and date functions, disk management procedures, program lister, cross reference utility, tracer utility and more. 221 pp
ISBN 0-916439-30-5　　　　　　$19.95
Canada: 52088 $25.95

To order direct call Toll Free 1-800-451-4319
In US and Canada add $4.00 shipping and handling. Foreign orders add $12.00 per item. Michigan residents add 4% sales tax

PC Training Kits

Learn to use MS-DOS, Lotus 1•2•3 or WordPerfect at your own pace, using one of these proven training packages.

Each package provides all the materials you'll need to teach yourself one of these PC applications. Our series includes the most popular applications: MS-DOS, Lotus 1-2-3, and WordPerfect, with others planned. The PC Training Kit will have you using your application in no time at all. These kits were designed and produced by experts in their respective fields: Professional trainers, Video producers, Book publishers, Script writers and public speakers. So you will have the additional experience of writers who have carefully tailored these courses for the student who wants to become more productive sooner.

Here's what you'll find in each package:

Workbook: A course workbook reinforces the training course contents. Learning theory tells us that immediate reinforcement, such as a course workbook, can encourage more in-depth learning.

Program Reference Guide: A complete Program Reference Guide. This is a compact, hardcover reference book that will serve you for years. It has all of the commands and details about your particular PC application. After you complete the training course, you can refer to this PRG for further information.

Computer Glossary: A valuable computer glossary designed to familiarize you with common computer terms and abbreviations. The computer world is filled with hi-tech jargon, this glossary helps you to understand it.

Reference Card: A handy desktop reference card. Put this convenient card next to your computer and you will always have the information you need close at hand.

Video Cassette: A 40 minute video training course covering introductory and intermediate level concepts, techniques and commands. The contents are based on course seminars for thousands of PC users and is scripted by professional writers with years of broadcast experience.

Suggested Retail Price: $175.00

To order direct call Toll Free 1-800-451-4319
In US and Canada add $4.00 shipping and handling. Foreign orders add $12.00 per item. Michigan residents add 4% sales tax

Abacus Order Form

Qty.	PC Books	Price	Companion Disk Qty.	Companion Disk Price	Subtotal
	Beginners Series				
	COBOL for Beginners	$18.95		$14.95	
	dBASE IV for Beginners	18.95		N/A	
	Excel for Beginners	18.95		N/A	
	GW-BASIC Programming for Beginners	18.95		14.95	
	Lotus 1-2-3 for Beginners	18.95		N/A	
	Microsoft Word for Beginners	18.95		N/A	
	Microsoft Works for Beginners	18.95		N/A	
	MS-DOS for Beginners	18.95		N/A	
	PC and Compatible Computers for Beginners	18.95		N/A	
	Unix for Beginners	18.95		N/A	
	Ventura Publisher for Beginners	18.95		14.95	
	Developers Series				
	PC System Programming for Developers	$39.95		$20.00	
	PC System Programming for Developers	59.95		Included	
	File Formats & Conversions for Developers	34.95		Included	
	Graphic Card Programming for Developers	34.95		Included	
	Turbo Pascal Internals for Developers	49.95		Included	
	Productivity Series				
	Complete Guide to the Atari Portfolio	$17.95		N/A	
	MS-DOS Tips & Tricks	17.95		N/A	
	Printer Tips & Tricks	34.95		Included	
	PC Tools Complete	22.95		N/A	
	Quick Reference Books (Hardcover)				
	dBASE III Plus & IV Reference Guide	$9.95		N/A	
	GW-BASIC Program Reference Guide	9.95		N/A	
	Lotus 1-2-3 Program Reference Guide	9.95		N/A	
	Multiplan Word Program Reference Guide	9.95		N/A	
	MS-DOS Program Reference Guide	9.95		N/A	
	PC Tools Companion	12.95		N/A	
	UNIX & XENIX Reference Guide (Softcover)	12.95		N/A	
	WordPerfect Program Reference Guide	9.95		N/A	

Continued..

Abacus Order Form cont.

Qty.	Miscellanious PC Books	Price	Companion Disk Qty.	Companion Disk Price	Subtotal
	Computer Viruses - A High-Tech Disease	$18.95	N/A		
	Science & Enineering. Applications	19.95		14.95	
	Turbo Pascal Tricks & Tips	19.95		14.95	

Payment:
- ☐ Visa
- ☐ Master Card
- ☐ Am. Express
- ☐ Check
- ☐ Money Order

Subtotal	
Michigan residents add 4% sales tax	
In US add $4.00 Postage per order	
Foreign orders add $12.00 per item	
TOTAL amount enclosed (U.S. funds)	

Card No. _____ Exp. Date _____

For fast delivery Order Toll Free 1-800-451-4319

Name _____

Address _____

City _____

State _____ Country _____ Zip _____

Phone _____

Send your completed order blank to:
Abacus
5370 52nd Street SE
Grand Rapids, MI 49512

Your order will be shipped within 24 hours of our receiving it. For extra-fast service order by phone with your credit card. Call Toll Free: 1-800-451-4319.
Prices and availability subject to change without notice.